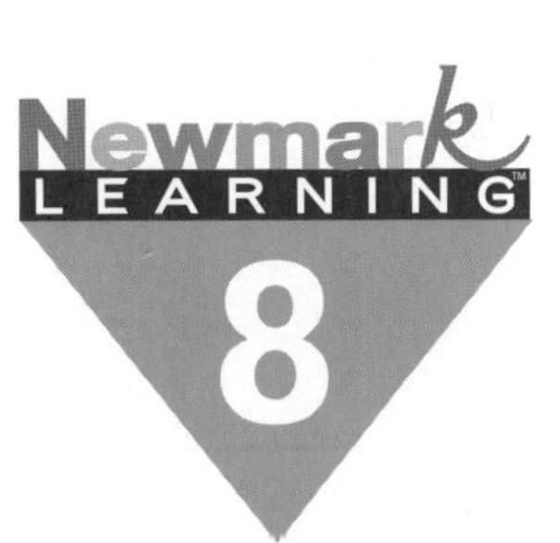

STAAR
Reading
Warm-Ups
&Test Practice

Newmark Learning
145 Huguenot Street • New Rochelle, NY • 10801

Editor: Jessica Pippin
Designer: Raquel Hernández
Illustrators: Brandon Fall, Caroline Romanet

Photo credits: Page 38A: Stuwdamdorp/Alamy; Page 93: Manuel Cohen Photography/Manuel Cohen/Newscom

ISBN: 978-1-4788-0744-5

Table of Contents

Contents	Page
Introduction	4
Warm-Up 1 Fiction: from *Heidi* by Johanna Spyri 8.2(B), 8.6(A), 8.6(C), 8.6 Fig. 19(D)	15
Warm-Up 2 Science Text: Weather Patterns 8.2(E), 8.10(A), 8.10(C), 8.13(A)	19
Warm-Up 3 Drama: from *The Post Office* by Rabindranath Tagore 8.3(C), 8.5(A), 8.5 Fig. 19(D)	23
Warm-Up 4 Social Studies Text: The Bone Wars 8.2(A), 8.10(A), 8.10(B), 8.10 Fig. 19(D)	29
Warm-Up 5 Realistic Fiction: An Unexpected Treasure 8.2(B), 8.6(A), 8.6(B), 8.6 Fig. 19(D)	33
Warm-Up 6 Procedural/How-To: How to Fix a Flat Bike Tire 8.2(E), 8.12(B), 8.12 Fig. 19(D)	37
Warm-Up 7 Fiction: from *The Adventures of Tom Sawyer*, Chapter 3 by Mark Twain 8.3(C), 8.6(A), 8.6(B), 8.6(C), 8.8(A)	41
Warm-Up 8 Science Text: The Storytelling Canyon 8.2(A), 8.10(A), 8.10(C), 8.10(D), 8.13(C)	45
Warm-Up 9 Literary Nonfiction: from "Advice to Youth" by Mark Twain 8.2(A), 8.7(A), 8.7 Fig. 19(D), 8.7 Fig. 19(E)	49
Warm-Up 10 Social Studies Text: Endurance 8.2(B), 8.10(B), 8.10(C), 8.10 Fig. 19(D), 8.13(C)	53
Practice Test 1 Poetry: from "The Wreck of the Hesperus" by H.W. Longfellow Poetry: "I Wandered Lonely As a Cloud" by William Wordsworth 8.3(C), 8.3 Fig. 19(D), 8.4(A), 8.4 Fig. 19(D), 8.4 Fig. 19(E), 8.8(A)	57
Practice Test 2 Speech: from The "Iron Curtain" Speech by Winston Churchill Speech: from President Ronald Reagan's Address to the British Parliament (1982) 8.2(E), 8.9(A), 8.11(A), 8.11(B), 8.11 Fig. 19(D), 8.11 Fig. 19(E) 8.11 Fig. 19(F)	65
Practice Test 3 Historical Fiction: The Blacksmith's Helper Legend: How Moccasins Were Made 8.2(B), 8.3(A), 8.3(C), 8.6(A), 8.6(B), 8.6(C), 8.6 Fig. 19(D), 8.6 Fig. 19(F), 8.8(A), 8.10(A) 8.13(A)	71
Practice Test 4 Social Studies Text: Constructing a Monument: Stonehenge Social Studies Text: Sister of Stonehenge 8.2(A), 8.2(B), 8.9(A), 8.10(A), 8.10(C), 8.10(D), 8.10 Fig. 19(D), 8.10 Fig. 19(F), 8.13(A), 8.13(C)	81
Practice Test 5 Myth: Prometheus the Fire Giver Myth: How Maui Brought Fire to the World 8.2(B), 8.3(A), 8.3(B), 8.3(C), 8.6(A), 8.6(B), 8.6 Fig. 19(D), 8.6 Fig. 19(F)	91
Answer Key	101

Introduction

STAAR Reading Warm-Ups & Test Practice is designed to prepare students for the STAAR Reading Tests. The STAAR Reading Assessments, administered every spring to students in Grades 3–8, assess students' ability to:

- Use text evidence to support ideas about texts
- Develop analytical skills in multiple text genres
- Use reading strategies to support making meaning from text
- Understand academic vocabulary

The goal of the STAAR Reading Tests is for students to read and understand a variety of literary and informational texts. In the reading exams, greater emphasis will be placed on critical analysis rather than literal understanding of texts.

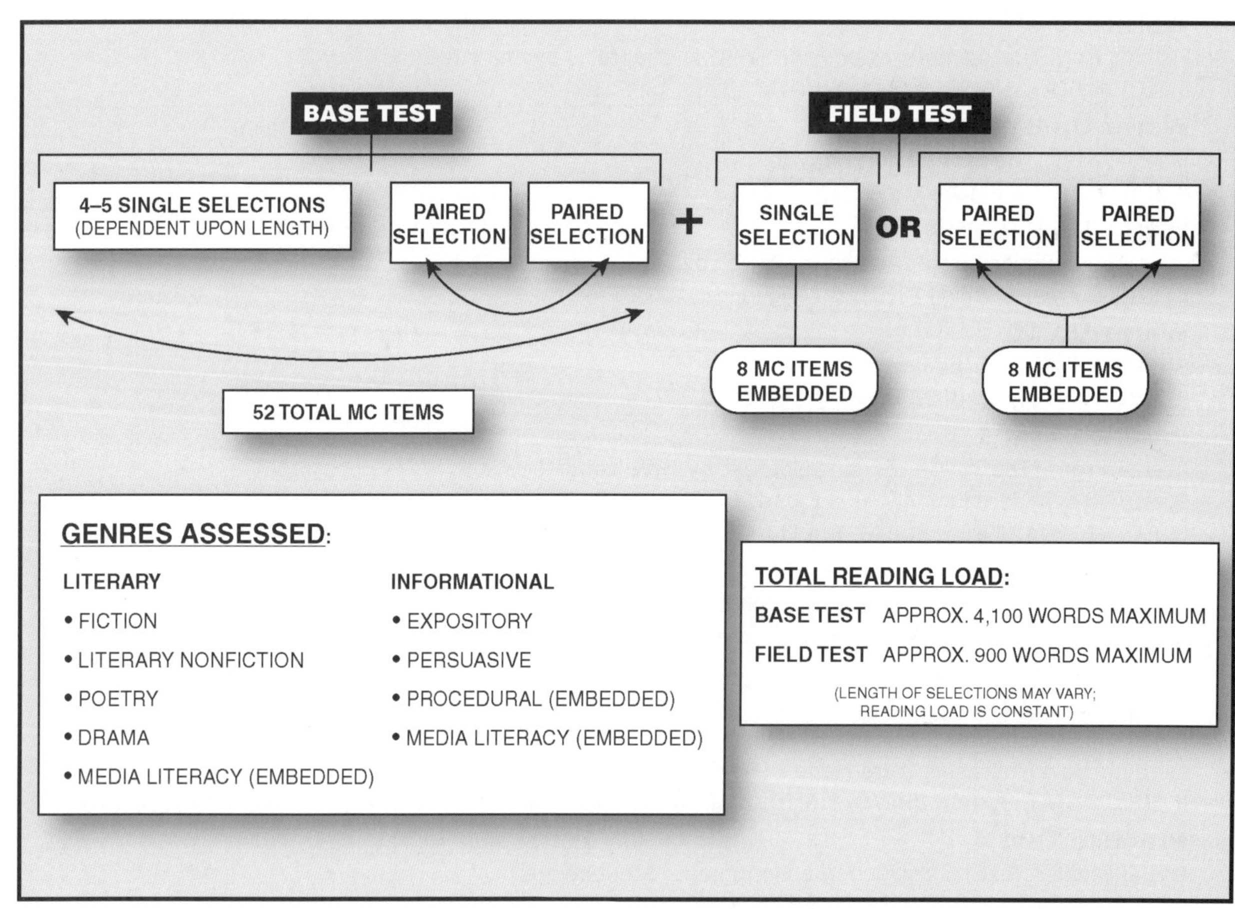

Readiness & Supporting Standards

The STAAR tests assess students based on specific Texas Essential Knowledge and Skills (TEKS). For each grade, the Texas Education Agency (TEA) has identified a set of knowledge and skills drawn from the TEKS. This set of knowledge and skills is known as **readiness standards**. These skills will be assessed and emphasized on the STAAR tests. Readiness standards make up 60%–70% of the STAAR Reading Test.

According to the TEA, readiness standards have the following characteristics:

- They are essential for success in the current grade or course.
- They are important for preparedness for the next grade or course.
- They support college and career readiness.
- They necessitate in-depth instruction.
- They address broad and deep ideas.

The remaining set of knowledge and skills is known as **supporting standards**. According to the TEA, they have the following characteristics:

- Although introduced in the current grade or course, they may be emphasized in a subsequent year.
- Although reinforced in the current grade or course, they may be emphasized in a previous year.
- They play a role in preparing students for the next grade or course but not a central role.
- They address more narrowly defined ideas.

A skills chart is included on page 12 of *STAAR Reading Warm-Ups & Test Practice.* A correlation chart that indicates what skills are covered in each question is included on page 14.

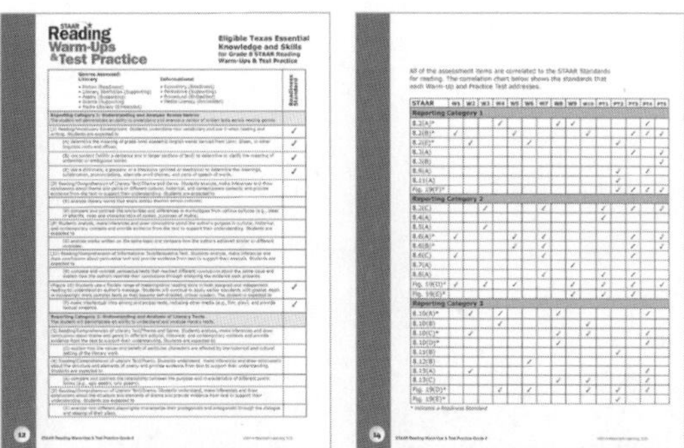

How are the STAAR Reading Tests structured?

The STAAR Reading Tests include 40 multiple-choice questions. Students will read four or five selections and answer a set of questions after each selection. Beginning in Grade 4, students might compare two selections and answer questions.

Specific features of the STAAR Reading Test include the following:

- The tests will have a four-hour time limit.
- Tests will be administered in paper format.
- STAAR will focus on the most critical TEKS, which will better measure the academic performance of students from elementary to middle school and eventually high school.
- All questions will be multiple-choice.

Reporting Categories	Number of Standards		Number of Questions	
Reporting Category 1: **Understanding/Analysis Across Genres**	Readiness Standards	4	10	
	Supporting Standards	4		
	Total	8		
Reporting Category 2: **Understanding/Analysis of Literary Texts**	Readiness Standards	4	22	
	Supporting Standards	10		
	Total	14		
Reporting Category 3: **Understanding/Analysis of Informational Texts**	Readiness Standards	5	20	
	Supporting Standards	7		
	Total	12		
Readiness Standards	**Total Number of Standards**	13	60%–70%	31–36
Supporting Standards	**Total Number of Standards**	21	30%–40%	16–21
Total Number of Questions on Test			52	

STAAR Reading Warm-Ups & Test Practice Grade 8

How will this book help students prepare?

STAAR Reading Warm-Ups & Test Practice is designed to help prepare students for the STAAR assessments. There are ten Warm-Ups and five Practice Tests.

Selections include every genre covered on the STAAR skills assessment. There is an assortment of literary and informational texts, including poetry and literary nonfiction. In the selections for Grade 8, the genres assessed are fiction, literary nonfiction, poetry, drama, media literacy, expository, persuasive, and procedural.

Tear-out answer keys for the Warm-Ups and Practice Tests are provided in the back, as well as sample bubble sheets for students to use while taking the tests.

Warm-Ups

STAAR Reading Warm-Ups & Test Practice includes ten Warm-Ups, which are short tests that are designed to provide students with an opportunity for quick, guided practice.

The ten Warm-Ups feature short reading selections that include examples of the genres that students are required to read in each grade level and will encounter on the test.

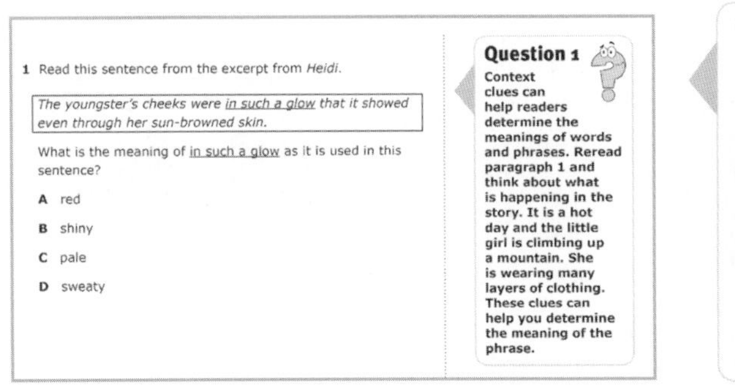

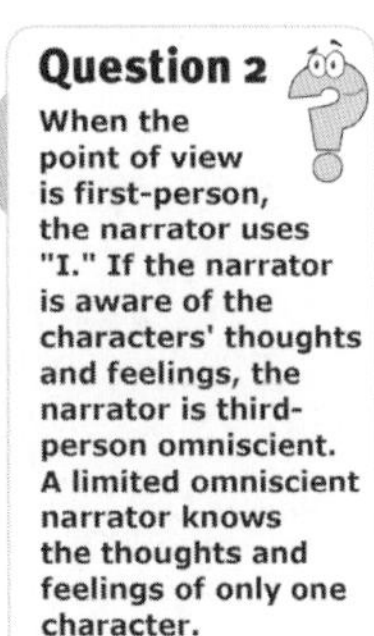

The Warm-Ups also include prompts with each question. These prompts are designed to guide students through the test. They model the thinking needed for answering questions, provide reading strategies, and include additional support for answering the questions. A variety of skills and standards are addressed in the Warm-Up prompts.

Practice Tests

The Practice Tests feature longer selections that match the selection lengths that will be used for the STAAR Assessments and the number of corresponding questions. These selections provide students with experience reading the longer and more complex texts they will have to read on the assessments.

Three of the Practice Tests also feature paired selections. Students are required to read paired selections in Grade 8. The Practice Tests are designed to be flexible. Students can take each test individually, or they can take a longer test featuring two selections and twice the number of questions.

The paired selections give students the opportunity to compare and contrast texts and integrate information from multiple texts, as required beginning in Grade 4.

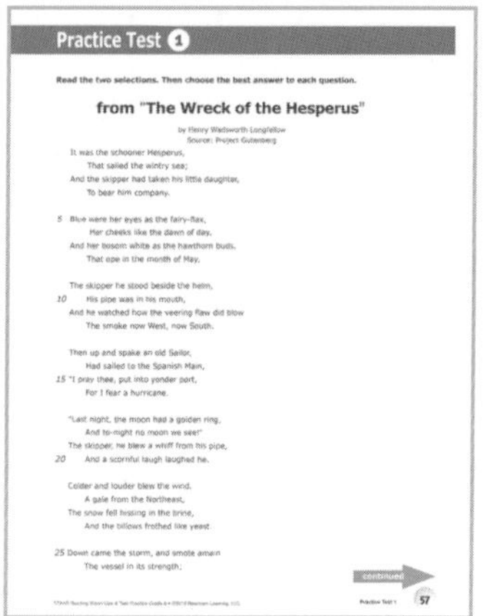

Literature

Informational Texts

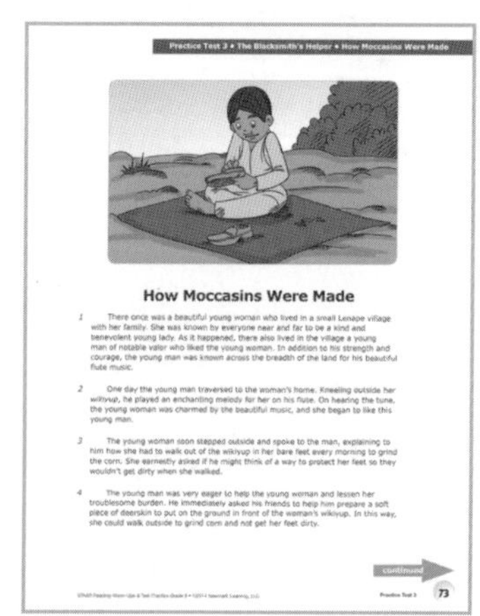

Paired Texts

STAAR Reading Warm-Ups & Test Practice Grade 8　　　　　　　　　©2014 Newmark Learning, LLC

Each selection is followed by a complete set of questions that reflect the number of questions students will find with each selection on the assessments. In addition, similar to the Warm-Ups, the Practice Tests also include the types of questions students will see on the assessments.

Questions with multiple answers

Tear-Out Answer Keys & Bubble Sheets

The answers to all the Warm-Ups and Practice Tests are provided in the Answer Key beginning on page 101. The Answer Key includes the standards correlations for each question.

Sample bubble sheets are provided on page 131. These bubble sheets resemble general answer sheets that students might use on a standardized test. They add to the authenticity of the test-taking experience and also allow students to practice filling out a bubble sheet.

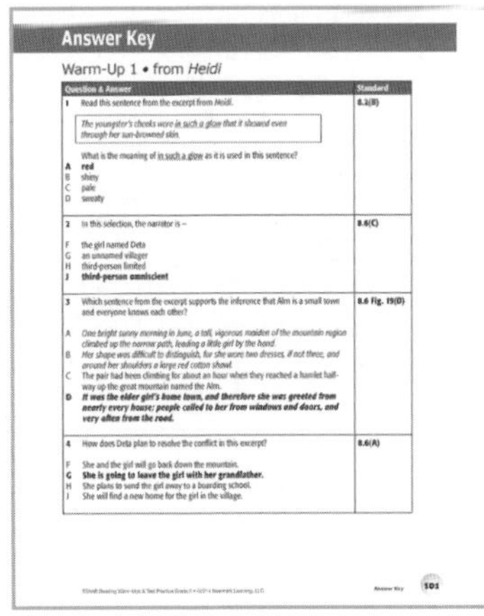

Answer Key

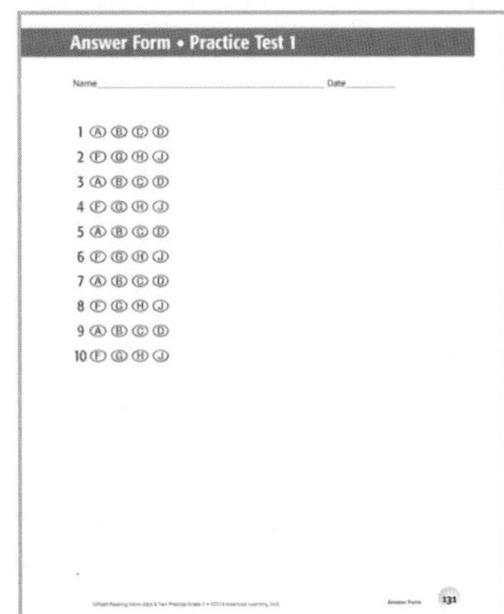

Answer Form

How to Use This Book

Warm-Ups

The Warm-Ups are designed to be quick and easy practice for students. They can be used in a variety of ways:

- Assign Warm-Ups for homework.

- Use them for quick review in class.

- Use them for targeted review of key standards. The correlation chart on page 14 can identify Warm-Ups that address the skills you want to focus on.

Practice Tests

The longer Practice Tests can be used to prepare students in the weeks before the assessments. They can also be used to assess students' reading comprehension throughout the year.

Test-Taking Experience

To simulate an actual STAAR Reading Test, choose two of the paired Practice Tests (15 questions each) and one of the single Practice Tests (10 questions each). This will create a 40-question test, which is how many questions are on the actual STAAR test. Use the sample bubble sheets in the back of the book, as well.

You may want to read the section below when introducing the test. This is similar to what is announced before each STAAR test.

> **Say:** *Today you will be taking the reading test of the State of Texas Assessments of Academic Readiness, or STAAR. It is important for you to do your best. If you have any questions or need any help, please raise your hand.*
>
> *I cannot help answer any test questions. I will be able to help you only with questions about the directions. If you do not know the answer to a question, choose the answer you think might be correct. Remember that you may write in your test booklet if you would like to make notes.*
>
> *You will now take the reading test by yourself. Remember to mark your answers very carefully and make your marks dark and neat. If there are no more questions, you may begin.*

Test-Taking Tips

Below are some helpful test-taking tips to consider before the STAAR Reading Test is administered.

- Be well rested the day of the test. It is important to eat a balanced breakfast the morning of the test.

- Begin the morning of the test with a positive attitude and confidence. Try to remain relaxed throughout the test.

- Have all materials ready before the test begins: pencil, eraser, and any other required materials.

- Be aware of how the test is structured so there are no surprises when the exam begins.

- Manage time. Taking practice exams, such as the ones provided in *STAAR Reading Warm-Ups & Test Practice*, will help you learn how to pace yourself and complete all answers in the allotted time.

- STAAR Reading Assessments are all multiple-choice. Cross out incorrect answers and use the process of elimination to figure out the correct answer.

- Many of the answers can be found in the text. Go back to each passage and underline important parts.

- Fill in the answer sheet carefully, leaving no stray pencil marks.

- If finished early, go back through the test and check over the answers. It is never good to rush through an exam.

	Readiness Standard
Genres Assessed: **Literary** • Fiction (Readiness) • Literary Nonfiction (Supporting) • Poetry (Supporting) • Drama (Supporting • Media Literacy (Embedded) **Informational** • Expository (Readiness) • Persuasive (Supporting) • Procedural (Embedded) • Media Literacy (Embedded)	
Reporting Category 1: Understanding and Analysis Across Genres The student will demonstrate an ability to understand and analyze a variety of written texts across reading genres.	
(2) Reading/Vocabulary Development. Students understand new vocabulary and use it when reading and writing. Students are expected to	✓
(A) determine the meaning of grade-level academic English words derived from Latin, Greek, or other linguistic roots and affixes;	✓
(B) use context (within a sentence and in larger sections of text) to determine or clarify the meaning of unfamiliar or ambiguous words;	✓
(E) use a dictionary, a glossary, or a thesaurus (printed or electronic) to determine the meanings, syllabication, pronunciations, alternate word choices, and parts of speech of words.	✓
(3) Reading/Comprehension of Literary Text/Theme and Genre. Students analyze, make inferences and draw conclusions about theme and genre in different cultural, historical, and contemporary contexts and provide evidence from the text to support their understanding. Students are expected to	
(A) analyze literary works that share similar themes across cultures;	
(B) compare and contrast the similarities and differences in mythologies from various cultures (e.g., ideas of afterlife, roles and characteristics of deities, purposes of myths).	
(9) Students analyze, make inferences and draw conclusions about the author's purpose in cultural, historical, and contemporary contexts and provide evidence from the text to support their understanding. Students are expected to	
(A) analyze works written on the same topic and compare how the authors achieved similar or different purposes.	
(11) Reading/Comprehension of Informational Text/Persuasive Text. Students analyze, make inferences and draw conclusions about persuasive text and provide evidence from text to support their analysis. Students are expected to	
(A) compare and contrast persuasive texts that reached different conclusions about the same issue and explain how the authors reached their conclusions through analyzing the evidence each presents.	
(Figure 19) Students use a flexible range of metacognitive reading skills in both assigned and independent reading to understand an author's message. Students will continue to apply earlier standards with greater depth in increasingly more complex texts as they become self-directed, critical readers. The student is expected to	✓
(F) make intertextual links among and across texts, including other media (e.g., film, play), and provide textual evidence.	✓
Reporting Category 2: Understanding and Analysis of Literary Texts The student will demonstrate an ability to understand and analyze literary texts.	
(3) Reading/Comprehension of Literary Text/Theme and Genre. Students analyze, make inferences and draw conclusions about theme and genre in different cultural, historical, and contemporary contexts and provide evidence from the text to support their understanding. Students are expected to	
(C) explain how the values and beliefs of particular characters are affected by the historical and cultural setting of the literary work.	
(4) Reading/Comprehension of Literary Text/Poetry. Students understand, make inferences and draw conclusions about the structure and elements of poetry and provide evidence from text to support their understanding. Students are expected to	
(A) compare and contrast the relationship between the purpose and characteristics of different poetic forms (e.g., epic poetry, lyric poetry).	
(5) Reading/Comprehension of Literary Text/Drama. Students understand, make inferences and draw conclusions about the structure and elements of drama and provide evidence from text to support their understanding. Students are expected to	
(A) analyze how different playwrights characterize their protagonists and antagonists through the dialogue and staging of their plays.	
(6) Reading/Comprehension of Literary Text/Fiction. Students understand, make inferences and draw conclusions about the structure and elements of fiction and provide evidence from text to support their understanding. Students are expected to	✓

(A) analyze linear plot developments (e.g., conflict, rising action, falling action, resolution, subplots) to determine whether and how conflicts are resolved;	✓
(B) analyze how the central characters' qualities influence the theme of a fictional work and resolution of the central conflict;	✓
(C) analyze different forms of point of view, including limited versus omniscient, subjective versus objective.	
(7) Reading/Comprehension of Literary Text/Literary Nonfiction. Students understand, make inferences and draw conclusions about the varied structural patterns and features of literary nonfiction and provide evidence from text to support their understanding. Students are expected to	
(A) analyze passages in well-known speeches for the author's use of literary devices and word and phrase choice (e.g., aphorisms, epigraphs) to appeal to the audience.	
(8) Reading/Comprehension of Literary Text/Sensory Language. Students understand, make inferences and draw conclusions about how an author's sensory language creates imagery in literary text and provide evidence from text to support their understanding. Students are expected to	
(A) explain the effect of similes and extended metaphors in literary text.	
(13) Reading/Media Literacy. Students use comprehension skills to analyze how words, images, graphics, and sounds work together in various forms to impact meaning. Students will continue to apply earlier standards with greater depth in increasingly more complex texts. Students are expected to	
(A) evaluate the role of media in focusing attention on events and informing opinion on issues;	
(C) evaluate various techniques used to create a point of view in media and the impact on audience.	
(Figure 19) Reading/Comprehension Skills. Students use a flexible range of metacognitive reading skills in both assigned and independent reading to understand an author's message. Students will continue to apply earlier standards with greater depth in increasingly more complex texts as they become self-directed, critical readers. The student is expected to	✓
(D) make complex inferences about text and use textual evidence to support understanding;	✓
(E) summarize, paraphrase, and synthesize texts in ways that maintain meaning and logical order within a text and across texts.	✓
Reporting Category 3: Understanding and Analysis of Informational Texts The student will demonstrate an ability to understand and analyze informational texts.	
(10) Reading/Comprehension of Informational Text/Expository Text. Students analyze, make inferences and draw conclusions about expository text and provide evidence from text to support their understanding. Students are expected to	✓
(A) summarize the main ideas, supporting details, and relationships among ideas in text succinctly in ways that maintain meaning and logical order;	✓
(B) distinguish factual claims from commonplace assertions and opinions and evaluate inferences from their logic in text;	
(C) make subtle inferences and draw complex conclusions about the ideas in text and their organizational patterns;	✓
(D) synthesize and make logical connections between ideas within a text and across two or three texts representing similar or different genres and support those findings with textual evidence.	✓
(11) Reading/Comprehension of Informational Text/Persuasive Text. Students analyze, make inferences and draw conclusions about persuasive text and provide evidence from text to support their analysis. Students are expected to	
(B) analyze the use of such rhetorical and logical fallacies as loaded terms, caricatures, leading questions, false assumptions, and incorrect premises in persuasive texts.	
(12) Reading/Comprehension of Informational Text/Procedural Texts. Students understand how to glean and use information in procedural texts and documents. Students are expected to	
(B) evaluate graphics for their clarity in communicating meaning or achieving a specific purpose.	
(13) Reading/Media Literacy. Students use comprehension skills to analyze how words, images, graphics, and sounds work together in various forms to impact meaning. Students will continue to apply earlier standards with greater depth in increasingly more complex texts. Students are expected to	
(A) evaluate the role of media in focusing attention on events and informing opinion on issues;	
(C) evaluate various techniques used to create a point of view in media and the impact on audience.	
(Figure 19) Reading/Comprehension Skills. Students use a flexible range of metacognitive reading skills in both assigned and independent reading to understand an author's message. Students will continue to apply earlier standards with greater depth in increasingly more complex texts as they become self-directed, critical readers. The student is expected to	✓
(D) make complex inferences about text and use textual evidence to support understanding;	✓
(E) summarize, paraphrase, and synthesize texts in ways that maintain meaning and logical order within a text and across texts.	✓

All of the assessment items are correlated to the STAAR Standards for reading. The correlation chart below shows the standards that each Warm-Up and Practice Test addresses.

STAAR	W1	W2	W3	W4	W5	W6	W7	W8	W9	W10	PT1	PT2	PT3	PT4	PT5
Reporting Category 1															
8.2(A)*				✓				✓	✓					✓	
8.2(B)*	✓				✓					✓			✓	✓	✓
8.2(E)*		✓				✓						✓			
8.3(A)													✓		✓
8.3(B)															✓
8.9(A)												✓		✓	
8.11(A)												✓			
Fig. 19(F)*												✓	✓	✓	✓
Reporting Category 2															
8.3(C)			✓				✓				✓		✓		✓
8.4(A)											✓				
8.5(A)			✓												
8.6(A)*	✓				✓		✓						✓		✓
8.6(B)*					✓		✓						✓		✓
8.6(C)	✓						✓						✓		
8.7(A)									✓						
8.8(A)							✓					✓		✓	
Fig. 19(D)*	✓		✓		✓					✓		✓		✓	✓
Fig. 19(E)*										✓		✓			
Reporting Category 3															
8.10(A)*		✓		✓					✓					✓	
8.10(B)				✓							✓				
8.10(C)*		✓							✓		✓			✓	
8.10(D)*									✓					✓	
8.11(B)												✓			
8.12(B)					✓										
8.13(A)		✓												✓	
8.13(C)									✓		✓			✓	
Fig. 19(D)*				✓		✓					✓		✓	✓	
Fig. 19(E)*													✓		

indicates a Readiness Standard

STAAR
STATE OF TEXAS ASSESSMENTS OF ACADEMIC READINESS

8.2(B)
Use context (within a sentence and in larger sections of text) to determine or clarify the meaning of unfamiliar or ambiguous words or words with novel meanings.

8.6(A)
Analyze linear plot developments (e.g., conflict, rising action, falling action, resolution, subplots) to determine whether and how conflicts are resolved.

8.6(C)
Analyze different forms of point of view, including limited versus omniscient, subjective versus objective.

Fig. 19(D)
Make complex inferences about text and use textual evidence to support understanding.

Read the selection and choose the best answer to each question.

from *Heidi*

by Johanna Spyri

1   One bright sunny morning in June, a tall, vigorous maiden of the mountain region climbed up the narrow path, leading a little girl by the hand. The youngster's cheeks were <u>in such a glow</u> that it showed even through her sun-browned skin. Small wonder though! for in spite of the heat, the little one, who was scarcely five years old, was bundled up as if she had to brave a bitter frost. Her shape was difficult to distinguish, for she wore two dresses, if not three, and around her shoulders a large red cotton shawl. With her feet encased in heavy hob-nailed boots, this hot and shapeless little person toiled up the mountain.

2   The pair had been climbing for about an hour when they reached a hamlet half-way up the great mountain named the Alm. It was the elder girl's home town, and therefore she was greeted from nearly every house; people called to her from windows and doors, and very often from the road. But, answering questions and calls as she went by, the girl did not loiter on her way and only stood still when she reached the end of the hamlet. There a few cottages lay scattered about, from the furthest of which a voice called out to her through an open door:

3   "Wait a moment, Deta, I'll go with you, if you are bound up the mountain."

continued

4   A stout, pleasant-looking woman stepped out of the house and joined the two.

5   "Where are you taking the child, Deta?" asked the newcomer. "Is she the child your sister left?"

6   "Yes," Deta assured her; "I am taking her up to the Alm-Uncle and there I want her to remain."

7   "You can't really mean to take her there, Deta. You must have lost your senses, to go to him. I am sure the old man will show you the door and won't even listen to what you say."

8   "Why not? As he's her grandfather, it is high time he should do something for the child. I have taken care of her until this summer and now a good place has been offered to me. The child shall not hinder me from accepting it, I tell you that!"

Name____ Date__________

1 Read this sentence from the excerpt from *Heidi*.

> *The youngster's cheeks were <u>in such a glow</u> that it showed even through her sun-browned skin.*

What is the meaning of <u>in such a glow</u> as it is used in this sentence?

A red

B shiny

C pale

D sweaty

---

2 In this selection, the narrator is —

F the girl named Deta

G an unnamed villager

H third-person limited

J third-person omniscient

Question 1

Context clues can help readers determine the meanings of words and phrases. Reread paragraph 1 and think about what is happening in the story. It is a hot day and the little girl is climbing up a mountain. She is wearing many layers of clothing. These clues can help you determine the meaning of the phrase.

Question 2

When the point of view is first-person, the narrator uses "I." If the narrator is aware of the characters' thoughts and feelings, the narrator is third-person omniscient. A limited omniscient narrator knows the thoughts and feelings of only one character.

continued

Name____ Date___________

Question 3 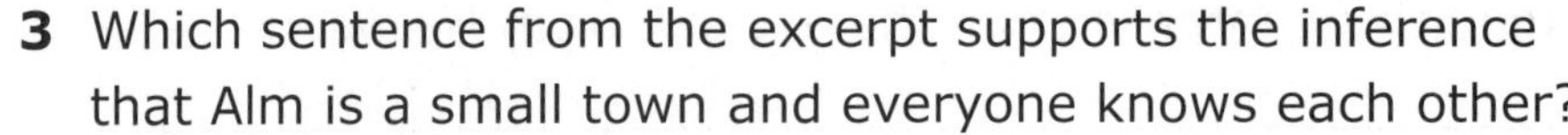

An inference is a logical guess readers can make based on details in the text. Read each piece of supporting evidence and ask yourself what you can infer from it. Then look for your inference in the list.

3 Which sentence from the excerpt supports the inference that Alm is a small town and everyone knows each other?

A *One bright sunny morning in June, a tall, vigorous maiden of the mountain region climbed up the narrow path, leading a little girl by the hand.*

B *Her shape was difficult to distinguish, for she wore two dresses, if not three, and around her shoulders a large red cotton shawl.*

C *The pair had been climbing for about an hour when they reached a hamlet half-way up the great mountain named the Alm.*

D *It was the elder girl's home town, and therefore she was greeted from nearly every house; people called to her from windows and doors, and very often from the road.*

Question 4

What is the conflict in this selection? Reread paragraphs 5–7. Based on the conversation between Deta and the woman, what does Deta plan to do with the child?

4 How does Deta plan to resolve the conflict in this excerpt?

F She and the girl will go back down the mountain.

G She is going to leave the girl with her grandfather.

H She plans to send the girl away to a boarding school.

J She will find a new home for the girl in the village.

Read the selection and choose the best answer to each question.

Weather Patterns

from NOAA's Weather and Atmosphere website

1   While a heat <u>wave</u> or a rainy week may cause discomfort for most of us, to a meteorologist they are fascinating examples of weather patterns, or repeating weather. Air masses affect the local weather on a daily and weekly basis. Jet streams carry the air from these masses to different parts of the country.

2   A jet stream is a narrow river of very strong winds that forms when two air masses with significant differences in temperature meet. The larger the temperature difference, the stronger the jet stream. A jet stream flows along the upper boundaries of these air masses and usually moves from west to east in a generally straight direction. Typically, jet stream winds affect the temperatures and precipitation for a few days. However, in some circumstances, the temperature difference in the air masses is less extreme, causing the jet stream to become sluggish and meander more north and south, forming a longer-term weather pattern. One example of this occurred in 2011, when Wichita Falls, Texas, had fifty-two consecutive days above 100°F.

8.2(E)
Use a dictionary, a glossary, or a thesaurus (printed or electronic) to determine the meanings, syllabication, pronunciations, alternate word choices, and parts of speech of words.

8.10(A)
Summarize the main ideas, supporting details, and relationships among ideas in text succinctly in ways that maintain meaning and logical order.

8.10(C)
Make subtle inferences and draw complex conclusions about the ideas in text and their organizational patterns.

8.13(A)
Evaluate the role of media in focusing attention on events and informing opinion on issues.

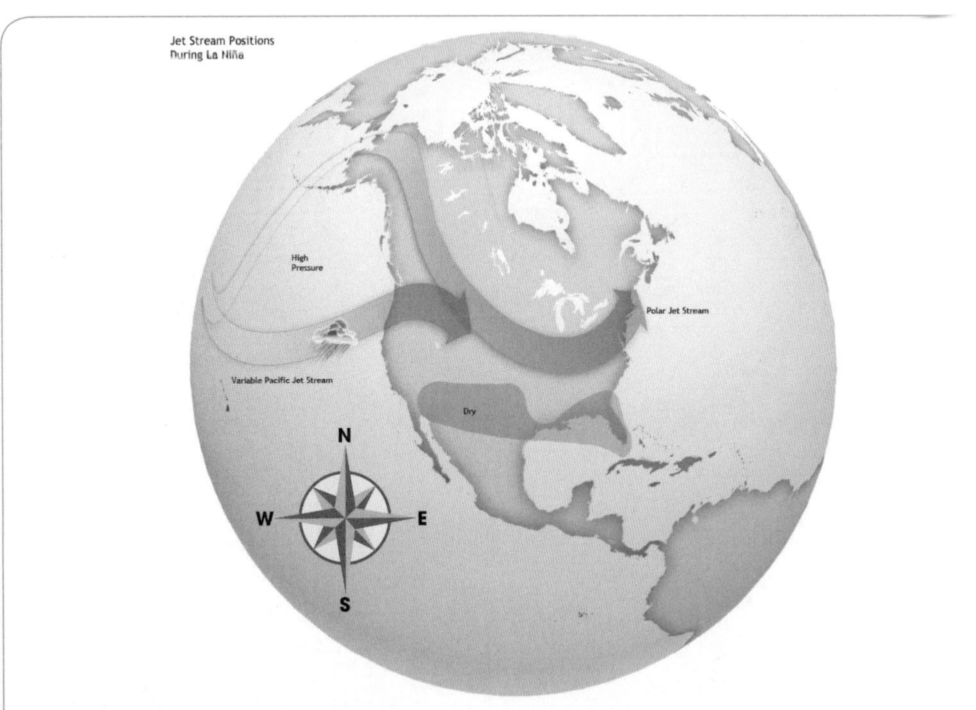

This diagram shows the paths of the jet streams during La Niña.

continued →

3   Every three to seven years, Earth has a weather pattern known as "El Niño." El Niño is the warming of the equatorial waters of the Pacific Ocean caused by a stronger, more southerly flowing jet stream. As a result, in the United States, the south experiences a wetter winter. Meanwhile, the west is stormier and the north is warmer. There is also an event called "La Niña" in which the equatorial waters of the Pacific Ocean cool. During La Niña, the jet stream shifts north, creating snowy winters and hot, dry summers in the north.

4   So the next time you are upset about the weather, take consolation in thinking like a meteorologist. See if you can identify a pattern that may be forming.

Name____ Date___________

1 Read the dictionary entry.

> **wave** \wāv\ *noun*
> **1.** a moving ridge or swell of water on a sea or lake **2.** a widespread movement of people or animals **3.** a greeting made with the hand **4.** a period of unusually hot or cold weather

Which definition of <u>wave</u> is used in paragraph 1?

A   Definition 1

B   Definition 2

C   Definition 3

D   Definition 4

Question 1

When you see a word that has more than one meaning, you can use context clues to figure out its meaning in the text you are reading. In this case, think about what this passage is about. Does definition 2 or 3 have anything to do with this selection?

---

2 Based on the information in this selection, the reader can conclude that —

F   air masses form only over land

G   understanding jet streams can help people predict local weather

H   jet streams form only in the United States

J   each of Earth's oceans causes different weather patterns

Question 2

An inference is a logical guess a reader makes based on details in the text. An inference can help you reach a conclusion. Skim the passage and look for a detail to support each answer choice. If there is no supporting detail, you can eliminate it as an answer choice.

continued

Name____ Date___________

Question 3

Reread paragraph 2. Think about what this paragraph is about, rather than the selection as a whole. What is the main idea discussed in this paragraph? The main idea should have supporting details.

3 What is paragraph 2 mainly about?

A Air masses are carried around the country by jet streams.

B In 2011, it was above 100°F for 52 days in a row in Wichita Falls, Texas.

C Jet streams are strong winds caused by temperature differences between air masses.

D Small temperature differences between air masses lead to longer weather patterns.

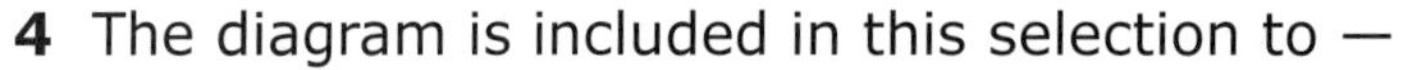

Question 4

When a passage includes a diagram or another type of text feature, think about how the text feature fits in with the passage. Why did the author include this with the text? What information does it have that you would not have learned otherwise?

4 The diagram is included in this selection to —

F describe the cause of storms in the United States

G illustrate the flow of the jet streams

H show the location of La Niña in the Pacific Ocean

J explain the differences in air temperatures

STAAR
STATE OF TEXAS ASSESSMENTS OF ACADEMIC READINESS

8.3(C)
Explain how the values and beliefs of particular characters are affected by the historical and cultural setting of the literary work.

8.5(A)
Analyze how different playwrights characterize their protagonists and antagonists through the dialogue and staging of their plays.

Fig. 19(D)
Make complex inferences about text and use textual evidence to support understanding.

Read the selection and choose the best answer to each question.

from *The Post Office*

by Rabindranath Tagore (1914)

CHARACTERS

AMAL: a boy

MADHAV: Amal's uncle

1   [*ACT I takes place in Madhav's house. The Physician has just left after telling Madhav that Amal is very ill and must not be allowed to go outside. MADHAV is standing alone in the front room as AMAL enters.*]

2   **AMAL** Uncle, I say, Uncle!

3   **MADHAV** Hullo! Is that you, Amal?

4   **AMAL** Mayn't I be out of the courtyard at all?

5   **MADHAV** No, my dear, no.

6   **AMAL** See, there where Auntie grinds lentils in the quirn, the squirrel is sitting with his tail up and with his wee hands he's picking up the broken grains of lentils and crunching them. Can't I run up there?

continued ➡

7   **MADHAV** No, my darling, no.

8   **AMAL** Wish I were a squirrel!—it would be lovely. Uncle, why won't you let me go about?

9   **MADHAV** Doctor says it's bad for you to be out.

10   **AMAL** How can the doctor know?

11   **MADHAV** What a thing to say! The doctor can't know and he reads such huge books!

12   **AMAL** Does his book-learning tell him everything?

13   **MADHAV** Of course, don't you know!

14   **AMAL** [*with a sigh*] Ah, I am so stupid! I don't read books.

15   **MADHAV** Now, think of it; very, very learned people are all like you; they are never out of doors.

16   **AMAL** Aren't they really?

17   **MADHAV** No, how can they? Early and late they toil and moil at their books, and they've eyes for nothing else. Now, my little man, you are going to be learned when you grow up; and then you will stay at home and read such big books, and people will notice you and say, "he's a wonder."

18   **AMAL** No, no, Uncle; I beg of you by your dear feet—I don't want to be learned, I won't.

19   **MADHAV** Dear, dear; it would have been my saving if I could have been learned.

20   **AMAL** No, I would rather go about and see everything that there is.

21   **MADHAV** Listen to that! See! What will you see, what is there so much to see?

22   **AMAL** See that far-away hill from our window—I often long to go beyond those hills and right away.

23   **MADHAV** Oh, you silly! As if there's nothing more to be done but just get up to the top of that hill and away! Eh! You don't talk sense, my boy. Now listen, since that hill stands there upright as a barrier, it means you can't get beyond it. Else, what was the use in heaping up so many large stones to make such a big affair of it, eh!

24   **AMAL** Uncle, do you think it is meant to prevent your crossing over? It seems to me because the earth can't speak it raises its hands into the sky and beckons. And those who live far and sit alone by their windows can see the signal. But I suppose the learned people—

25   **MADHAV** No, they don't have time for that sort of nonsense. They are not crazy like you.

26   **AMAL** Do you know, yesterday I met someone quite as crazy as I am.

27   **MADHAV** Gracious me, really, how so?

28   **AMAL** He had a bamboo staff on his shoulder with a small bundle at the top, and a brass pot in his left hand, and an old pair of shoes on; he was making for those hills straight across that meadow there. I called out to him and asked, "Where are you going?" He answered, "I don't know, anywhere!" I asked again, "Why are you going?" He said, "I'm going out to seek work." Say, Uncle, have you to seek work?

29   **MADHAV** Of course I have to. There's many about looking for jobs.

30   **AMAL** How lovely! I'll go about, like them too, finding things to do.

31   **MADHAV** Suppose you seek and don't find. Then—

32   **AMAL** Wouldn't that be jolly? Then I should go farther! I watched that man slowly walking on with his pair of worn out shoes. And when he got to where the water flows under the fig tree, he stopped and washed his feet in the stream. Then he took out from his bundle some gram-flour, moistened it with water and began to eat. Then he tied up his bundle and shouldered it again; tucked up his cloth above his knees and crossed the stream. I've asked Auntie to let me go up to the stream, and eat my gram-flour just like him.

33   **MADHAV** And what did your Auntie say to that?

34   **AMAL** Auntie said, "Get well and then I'll take you over there." Please, Uncle, when shall I get well?

35   **MADHAV** It won't be long, dear.

36   **AMAL** Really, but then I shall go right away the moment I'm well again.

continued

Name____ Date___________

Question 1

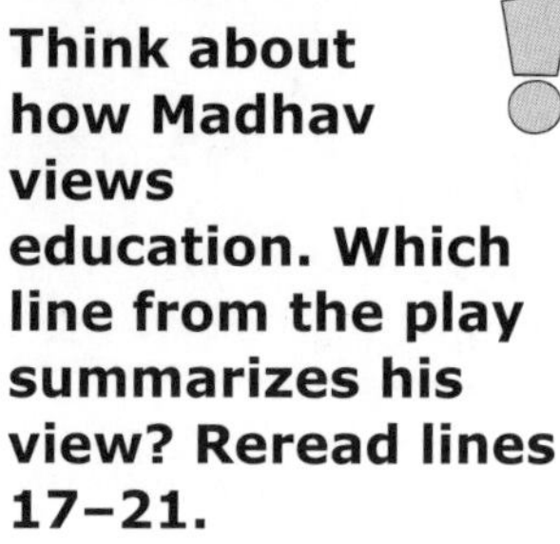

Stage directions can provide the setting, describe characters, and give background information about a play. What do the stage directions at the beginning of the play tell you?

1 In this play, what can the reader learn from the stage directions at the beginning?

A where Amal goes to school

B why the Physician has left

C what Madhav does for work

D why Amal cannot go outside

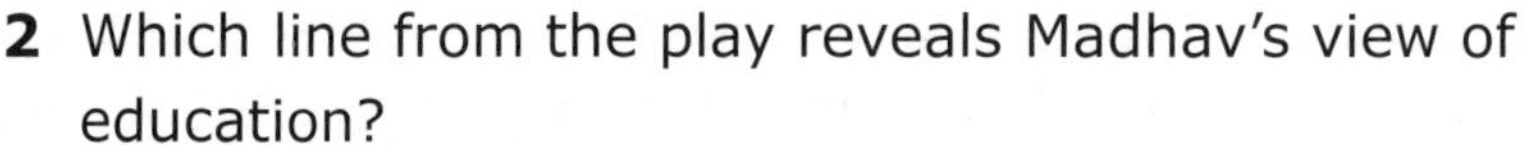

Question 2

Think about how Madhav views education. Which line from the play summarizes his view? Reread lines 17–21.

2 Which line from the play reveals Madhav's view of education?

F *Doctor says it's bad for you to be out.*

G *What a thing to say! The doctor can't know and he reads such huge books!*

H *Dear, dear; it would have been my saving if I could have been learned.*

J *Else, what was the use in heaping up so many large stones to make such a big affair of it, eh!*

Name____ Date___________

3 Which detail in the play shows that Madhav and Amal see things differently?

A Madhav sees the mountain as a barrier, but Amal sees it as an invitation.

B Madhav sees Amal's illness as a weakness, but Amal sees it as a strength.

C Madhav sees work as an exciting opportunity, but Amal sees it as a burden.

D Madhav sees the doctor as a fraud, but Amal sees him as an authority.

Question 3

Madhav and Amal disagree on many things in this play. Which answer choice best summarizes their disagreements? Reread the play, underlining the lines where Madhav and Amal disagree.

continued

Name____ Date__________

Question 4

Reread each answer choice. Then, go back through the play and find where Madhav and Amal discuss each one. Read Madhav's responses carefully, and find which answer choice best fits how society affects his views.

4 How does the society he lives in affect Madhav's views?

F He does not think the doctor has enough experience to diagnose illness.

G He believes it is very important for Amal to become learned.

H He wants Amal to leave home soon and experience different parts of the world.

J He thinks that Auntie, not his uncle, should take care of Amal.

STAAR
STATE OF TEXAS ASSESSMENTS OF ACADEMIC READINESS

8.2(A)
Determine the meaning of grade-level academic English words derived from Latin, Greek, or other linguistic roots and affixes.

8.10(A)
Summarize the main ideas, supporting details, and relationships among ideas in text succinctly in ways that maintain meaning and logical order.

8.10(B)
Distinguish factual claims from commonplace assertions and opinions and evaluate inferences from their logic in text.

Fig. 19(D)
Make complex inferences about text and use textual evidence to support understanding.

Read the selection and choose the best answer to each question.

The Bone Wars

1   One of the longest and most bitter rivalries in nineteenth-century America was not over gold, timber, or coal—but over dinosaur bones. Known as the Bone Wars, this fierce competition between two of the country's leading paleontologists not only caused each man to abhor the other, it also damaged the professional reputations of the two men.

2   In their quest to become known as the best of the dinosaur hunters, Othniel Charles Marsh and Edward Drinker Cope helped to discover more than 1,500 different types of fossils. For over twenty years, the two men engaged in a competition that was as bitter as it was fierce.

Edward Drinker Cope

Othniel Charles Marsh

continued

3   For both March and Cope, there were no measures too extreme or too outrageous in the race to become the reigning dinosaur hunter. They spied on each other's excavations. They bribed and bullied colleagues and workers. They even had their workers deliberately destroy fossils so the other man could not collect them. The contest between the two climaxed in 1877, with the discovery of fossils at two separate sites in Colorado. One site belonged to Marsh, the other to Cope. To Cope's dismay, Marsh would eventually uncover the first known remains of the dinosaurs *Stegosaurus* and *Brontosaurus*.

4   By 1892, the Bone Wars had come to an end. Their work had left both men almost penniless. However, the efforts of Cope and Marsh paid off handsomely in other ways; it is believed that more than 142 new species were discovered as a result of their work. It would appear that Marsh won the Bone Wars, with his discovery of some eighty new dinosaur fossils.

5   Although the relationship between Marsh and Cope was forever tainted, the findings by both men <u>galvanized</u> the American public's growing interest in dinosaurs, a fascination that continues to resonate more than a century later.

Name____ Date___________

1 Which sentence expresses a main idea of "The Bone Wars"?

A Competition between scientists in a field of study leads to handsome rewards.

B Scientific rivals encourage each other to do their best work.

C The rivalry between both Marsh and Cope had both positive and negative results.

D Colorado holds the most important dinosaur fossils found.

> **Question 1**
> A main idea is what a text is mostly about. Read each answer choice and determine where it is mentioned in the selection. If it is mentioned two or more times, it is likely a main idea.

2 Which detail from the selection supports the idea that Marsh and Cope would do anything to win the competition between them?

F *They even had their workers deliberately destroy fossils so the other man could not collect them.*

G *The contest between the two climaxed in 1877 with the discovery of fossils at two separate sites in Colorado.*

H *. . . it is believed that more than 142 new species were discovered as a result of their work.*

J *It would appear that Marsh won the Bone Wars with his discovery of some eighty new dinosaur fossils.*

> **Question 2**
> Did Marsh and Cope do anything that would prevent the other from winning the competition? Reread paragraph 3 in the selection, underlining the ways Marsh and Cope tried to win.

continued

Name____ Date___________

Question 3

A fact can be proven correct. You should be able to find a fact by talking to experts, or using encyclopedias, internet references, and nonfiction books. If these resources do not support a statement, that statement is probably an opinion.

3 Which sentence from the selection states a fact?

A *One of the longest and most bitter rivalries in nineteenth-century America was not over gold, timber, or coal—but over dinosaur bones.*

B *For over twenty years, the two men engaged in a competition that was as bitter as it was fierce.*

C *For both Marsh and Cope, there were no measures too extreme or too outrageous in the race to become the reigning dinosaur hunter.*

D *Marsh would eventually uncover the first known remains of the dinosaurs* Stegosaurus *and* Brontosaurus.

Question 4

To figure out the meaning of an unknown word, look for familiar Latin and Greek roots. Or, try replacing the word *galvanized* with each answer choice. Which option makes the most sense?

4 In paragraph 5, the word <u>galvanized</u> means —

F reduced; lessened

G stimulated; stirred

H dulled; dampened

J ridiculed; laughed at

Read the selection and choose the best answer to each question.

An Unexpected Treasure

1   As a little boy, Juan had spent many a night poring over books in his bed; he loved stories about buccaneers, brawls at sea, and full-sailed frigates cutting through endless ocean waters. When he wasn't fantasizing about life as a pirate, Juan was scouring the beaches of Mexico in hopes of finding buried treasure. As the years marched on, Juan became taller and wiser, yet he never outgrew his obsession. One sunny day, his wife presented him with a state-of-the-art metal detector and smiled broadly as Juan excitedly bounded out the door with it.

2   Juan strolled along the beach, running the end of his device over miles of sugar-white sand as hours passed by and the sun began its descent into the sea. Juan's stomach was grumbling, and he thought it was probably time to call it a day. Suddenly, he heard a beep. He flinched at the noise; he hadn't heard so much as a blip in all his hours <u>combing</u> the beach. With fingers trembling, Juan ran the disk of his metal detector back over the spot, straining his ears to hear the digital alarm sound out again. What a melodious tune it was: beep, beep, beep.

continued

3   Juan gave out a cry and picked up his shovel. He began to dig with a fervor he had never felt before. Before long, a small crowd formed around the perimeter of the growing hole, and people began to join in, using shovels or their bare hands. Juan dug and dug, his mind whirring with possibilities. Had he stumbled across a treasure chest filled with gold doubloons that had been buried centuries ago?

4   Juan's shovel struck something hard and unmoving. His eyes grew wide, he held his breath, and he scraped his hand across a thin metal placard that read: 093-BFX.

Name____ Date__________

1 The conflict in this story is resolved when Juan —

A finds a license plate buried in the sand

B decides to leave home and become a pirate

C becomes frustrated with the hunt along the beach

D learns how to work the metal detector at the end of the day

Question 1

Conflict happens in a story when the main character is trying to find a solution to a problem. What is Juan's problem, and how is it resolved? Reread paragraph 4.

2 In paragraph 2 of the story, the word <u>combing</u> means —

F tidying

G searching

H raking

J digging

Question 2

What is the root of *combing*? Use your knowledge of this root to figure out the meaning of the word *combing*.

continued

Name____ Date___________

Question 3

To describe a character, think about what the person says and does. Reread each answer choice. Think about Juan's character and how he behaves. What do his actions tell you about the character?

3 Juan finally finds something at the end of the day because he is —

A creative and enthusiastic

B patient and determined

C curious and imaginative

D angry and frustrated

Question 4

Use logic, reasoning, and observational skills to make an inference. An inference is something not explicitly written in a selection. You must use clues from the selection in order to reach a conclusion.

4 Which sentence from the story supports the inference that Juan's wife understands his obsession?

F *As the years marched on, Juan became taller and wiser, yet he never outgrew his obsession.*

G *One sunny day, his wife presented him with a state-of-the-art metal detector and smiled broadly as Juan excitedly bounded out the door with it.*

H *Juan strolled along the beach, running the end of his device over miles of sugar-white sand as hours passed by and the sun began its descent into the sea.*

J *With fingers trembling, Juan ran the disk of his metal detector back over the spot, straining his ears to hear the digital alarm sound out again.*

STAAR
STATE OF TEXAS ASSESSMENTS OF ACADEMIC READINESS

8.12(B)
Evaluate graphics for their clarity in communicating meaning or achieving a specific purpose.

Fig. 19(D)
Make complex inferences about text and use textual evidence to support understanding.

Read the selection and choose the best answer to each question.

How to Fix a Flat Bike Tire

Everyone loves to ride a bike, right? While it's great exercise to ride through the hills or around the neighborhood, a flat tire can quickly end the fun. Wherever you ride, you should have a tire repair kit and a small air pump with you just in case. Then you can get back on the road again with these simple steps.

Step 1: Remove the Wheel

In order to remove the wheel, release the brake first by spreading the brake pads. Then, depending on the type of wheel, undo the quick release lever or loosen the axle nut with a wrench until the wheel slides out.

Step 2: Find the Cause

Spin the wheel slowly to locate the cause of the leak. Look for a nail, a shard of glass, or other sharp object that may be lodged in the tire.

Step 3: Take the Tire Off the Rim

Use a tire lever, a flat <u>instrument</u> that can fit between the tire and the rim, to pry the wheel away from the rim. Run the lever all the way around between the rim and the tire to get one side of the tire off the rim. Once one side is off, it will be easy to grab the tire and pull it off.

Step 4: Remove the Tube from the Tire and Find Hole

Carefully take the tube out of the tire and examine it to locate the hole. (If you found the cause of the puncture in Step 2, then you may already know where the hole is.) If you cannot visually find the hole, there are a couple of other ways to find it: (a) pump some air into the tire and see if you can hear where the air is leaking out; or (b) fill a bucket with water and place each part of the tube under the water until you see a stream of bubbles coming from the leak.

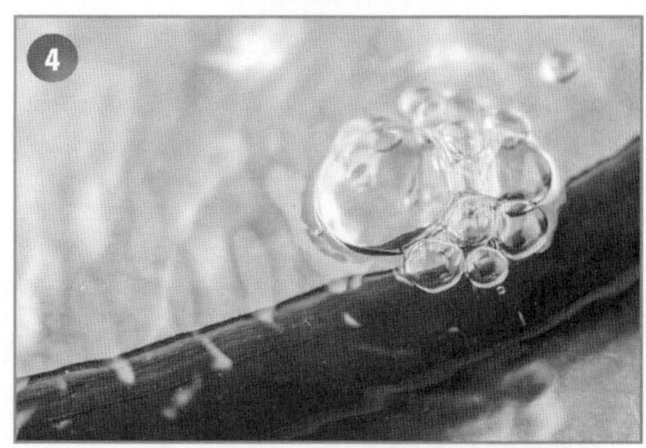

continued →

Step 5: Patch the Hole

Gently clean the area around the hole with sandpaper.
Make sure all dirt, dust, and rubber are removed so
the patch can stick properly. Apply a thin layer of
glue, using the tip of the glue tube to spread the glue
around, and then let the glue dry for 3–5 minutes. Put
the patch on top of the glue, making sure the puncture
is in the center of the patch.

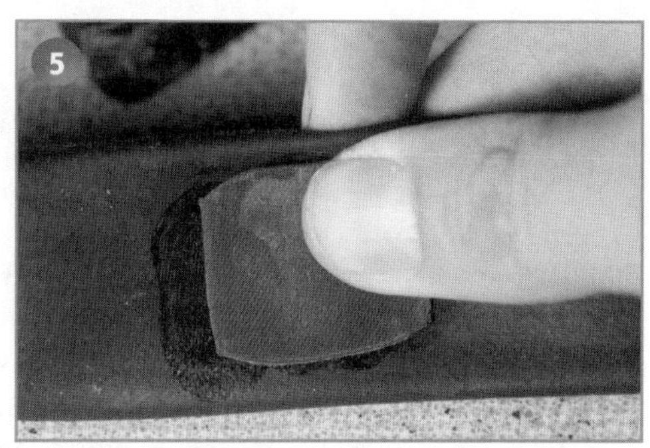

Step 6: Put the Tube Back in the Tire

Partially inflate the tube to make it easier to handle, and then put it back
inside the tire.

Step 7: Mount the Tire

Before remounting the tire, check the markings on the
side of the tire to make sure it will be turning in the
proper direction. In many cases, there will be an arrow
showing the direction the wheel should turn. Once
the tire is facing in the correct direction, put the valve
of the tube in the hole in the rim and then use your
hands to put the tire back on the rim. If it becomes
too difficult to put the tire back on, use the tire lever
to gently push the tire back onto the rim.

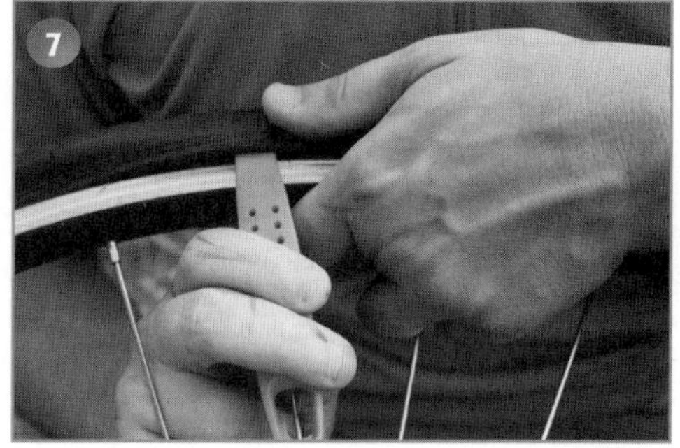

Step 8: Inflate and Insert

Inflate the tire to the correct pressure and put it back on the bike. Be sure
to check that the brakes are reconnected and that all releases are firmly
secured.

Name____ Date__________

1 Based on this selection, the reader can infer that a tire repair kit includes —

A a spare tube

B a set of wrenches

C glue and a patch

D new brake pads

> **Question 1**
>
> The selection does not explicitly state what would be in a repair kit. To figure this out, reread the selection and underline any of the tools and items you would need to repair a tire. Then, see which answer choices matches what you found.

2 What might be on a person's bike that is not shown in the first picture in this selection?

F tire

G rim

H brake pads

J axle nut

> **Question 2**
>
> Look at the first picture in this selection. Authors often include labeled images to help the reader understand a complex idea. Which parts of the bike are labeled? Which answer choice is not labeled?

continued

Name____ Date___________

Question 3

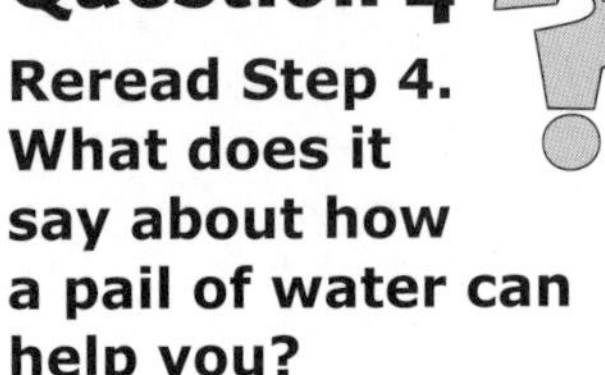

Images can provide helpful illustrations in how-to texts. Reread Step 3. What is it telling you to do? Look closely at the picture next to Step 3. How does it relate to the instructions in the text?

3 The picture next to Step 3 is included to show how to —

A find the leak

B use a tire lever

C patch the hole

D remove the tube

Question 4

Reread Step 4. What does it say about how a pail of water can help you?

4 When repairing a flat bike tire, a pail of water is useful for —

F washing the tire

G rinsing the brake pads

H locating the leak

J cleaning one's hands

Question 5

Read the different definitions of *instrument* carefully. Then think about what's happening in Step 3. Which answer choices can you eliminate immediately based on what the selection is about? Does playing musical instruments have anything to do with changing a bike tire?

5 Read the dictionary entry.

> **instrument** \in' strə mənt\ *noun*
> **1.** a mechanical tool or implement **2.** a device for producing musical sounds **3.** a device for measuring quantity or amount **4.** an agent or agency by which something is done, as in government programs

Which definition fits the word <u>instrument</u> in Step 3 of the selection?

A Definition 1

B Definition 2

C Definition 3

D Definition 4

Read the selection and choose the best answer to each question.

from *The Adventures of Tom Sawyer*, Chapter 3

by Mark Twain

In this excerpt, Tom Sawyer is painting his Aunt Polly's fence. His enthusiasm for the task quickly fades away.

1 But Tom's energy did not last. He began to think of the fun he had planned for this day, and his sorrows multiplied. Soon the free boys would come tripping along on all sorts of delicious expeditions, and they would make a world of fun of him for having to work—the very thought of it <u>burnt him like fire</u>.

2 He got out his worldly wealth and examined it—bits of toys, marbles, and trash; enough to buy an exchange of *work*, maybe, but not half enough to buy so much as half an hour of pure freedom. So he returned his straitened means to his pocket, and gave up the idea of trying to buy the boys. At this dark and hopeless moment an inspiration burst upon him! Nothing less than a great, magnificent inspiration.

STAAR

STATE OF TEXAS ASSESSMENTS OF ACADEMIC READINESS

8.3(C)
Explain how the values and beliefs of particular characters are affected by the historical and cultural setting of the literary work.

8.6(A)
Analyze linear plot developments (e.g., conflict, rising action, falling action, resolution, subplots) to determine whether and how conflicts are resolved.

8.6(B)
Analyze how the central characters' qualities influence the theme of a fictional work and resolution of the central conflict.

8.6(C)
Analyze different forms of point of view, including limited versus omniscient, subjective versus objective.

8.8(A)
Explain the effect of similes and extended metaphors in literary text.

continued ➡

3   He took up his brush and went tranquilly to work. Ben Rogers hove in sight presently—the very boy, of all boys, whose ridicule he had been dreading. Ben's gait was the hop-skip-and-jump—proof enough that his heart was light and his anticipations high. He was eating an apple, and giving a long, melodious whoop, at intervals, followed by a deep-toned ding-dong-dong, ding-dong-dong, for he was [im]personating a steamboat. As he drew near, he slackened speed, took the middle of the street, leaned far over to starboard and rounded to ponderously and with laborious pomp and circumstance—for he was [im]personating the Big Missouri, and considered himself to be drawing nine feet of water. He was boat and captain and engine-bells combined, so he had to imagine himself standing on his own hurricane-deck giving the orders and executing them.

Name____ Date___________

1 In this selection, the author included paragraph 2 in order to —

   A explain why Tom's enthusiasm for painting quickly faded away

   B show the reader that Tom has no money or valuables

   C reveal that Tom knows a lot of boys but has no real friends

   D let the reader know that Tom wants to get out of his situation

Question 1

Each paragraph in this excerpt has a purpose. What is the purpose of paragraph 2? What does it reveal to the reader about Tom's character?

2 The reader can conclude that when Tom sees Ben Rogers approaching, Tom feels —

   F amused

   G apprehensive

   H relieved

   J surprised

Question 2

Reread the last three sentences of paragraph 2. How does Tom feel when he sees Ben Rogers? What conclusion can you draw from Tom's reaction?

3 In paragraph 1, the phrase <u>burnt him like fire</u> suggests that Tom was —

   A resentful

   B satisfied

   C exhausted

   D sunburned

Question 3

Use context clues to help you determine the meaning of the phrase *burnt him like fire*. This phrase is also a simile, which compares two things using *like* or *as*.

continued

Name____ Date___________

Question 4

First, think about what point of view this story is from. Is it limited or omniscient? Based on the point of view, what information is revealed to you about the characters?

4 The narrative point of view in this story enables the reader to —

F predict what Ben Rogers will do next

G figure out that Tom Sawyer is an orphan

H identify the details of the setting

J understand Tom's thoughts and feelings

Question 5

Reread the story and underline any part that deals with the setting. Then think about what the characters are doing and how the setting might affect their actions.

5 Which of the characters' actions in this story is influenced by the setting?

A Tom finds pieces of toys and trash in his pocket.

B Tom decides to find someone else to do his work.

C Ben Rogers pretends to be on a steamboat on the river.

D Ben Rogers walks down the street eating a snack.

Read the selection and choose the best answer to each question.

The Storytelling Canyon

1   Each year, over five million people visit the formation known as the Grand Canyon. This geologic wonder, located in Arizona, fascinates scientists and tourists alike with its beauty and its size.

2   The canyon spans nearly three hundred miles long and as many as eighteen miles wide. In some places it reaches a fear-inducing one mile in depth. The massive cliffs, bold colors, and powerful river below are intriguing enough to make this landmark memorable, but its geological storytelling adds further significance. Erosion caused by the power of moving water formed the Grand Canyon. The Colorado River chiseled the canyon into Earth's crust. This expanse—the canyon—is a unique place where Earth's floor is literally split open, revealing countless years of the planet's history.

3   Geologists have found almost forty rock layers in the canyon's walls. These <u>strata</u> are a cross-section of approximately two billion years in Earth's history. Fossils, artifacts, and signs of little-known prehistoric eras are inlaid in these rocks. Evidence of volcanic activity streaks the walls as well, helping scientists identify dates for each rock layer they study.

continued ▶

4   Many of Earth's mysteries hide beneath its surface, buried too deep for scientists to access. For those who specialize in earlier periods of Earth's history, the Grand Canyon is a cherished resource. By studying the different rocks and fossils found in the canyon walls, scientists can access countless clues about the distant past. Time's many layers lie uncovered here, available to teach all they can.

5   Today, the canyon's monumental power continues to draw crowds. People come not only to be astonished and dazzled, but also to see a mile-deep time line of their planet's story, spelled out in jagged stripes and layers of history that may never be fully known.

Name____ Date___________

1 Which sentence expresses a main idea of this selection?

A The Grand Canyon is a popular tourist destination.

B The Grand Canyon reveals much about Earth's history.

C Many artifacts can be found in the rocks of the Grand Canyon.

D The Colorado River formed the Grand Canyon over millions of years.

Question 1

Sometimes, as with this passage, the main idea will not be stated in the introduction. When the main idea is not stated, look for an idea that is repeated in the body paragraphs. If an idea is repeated or referred to several times, it is most likely a main idea.

2 How is the central idea developed over the course of the selection?

F Each successive paragraph gives details from further back in Earth's history.

G Each successive paragraph gives a different reason why people visit the canyon.

H First the history of the canyon is described, and then the reasons why people visit the canyon are listed.

J First the formation of the canyon is described, and then the kind of evidence found in the canyon is outlined.

Question 2

How is this selection structured? Read each answer choice and look back at the selection to determine which one is correct.

continued

Name____ Date___________

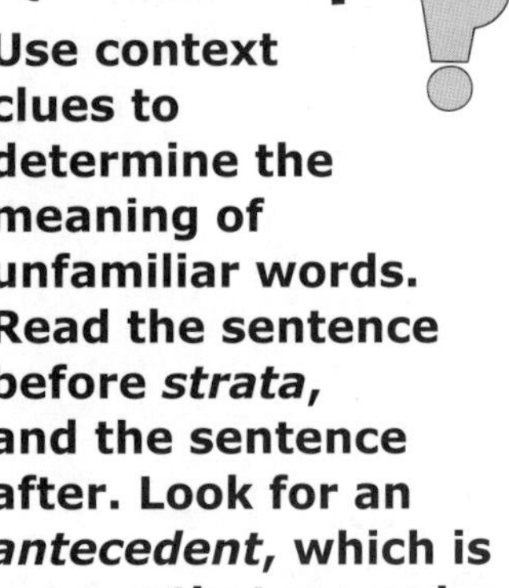

Question 3

Look through the passage for information on the Grand Canyon's size and what that size reveals about the canyon.

Question 4

Use context clues to determine the meaning of unfamiliar words. Read the sentence before *strata*, and the sentence after. Look for an *antecedent*, which is a noun that precedes another.

Question 5

In informational texts, images are often included to provide a visual for the reader. Think about what purpose this image serves in relation to the text.

3 What connection does "The Storytelling Canyon" make between the size of the Grand Canyon and its usefulness to scientists?

  A The depth of the canyon allows scientists to study the effects of water erosion on the land.

  B The depth of the canyon allows scientists to learn about distant periods in the history of Earth.

  C The length and width of the canyon allow scientists to examine many different types and colors of soil.

  D The length and width of the canyon allow scientists to study a large section of the surface of Earth.

4 Which phrase in paragraph 3 helps the reader understand the meaning of the word <u>strata</u>?

  F *rock layers*

  G *canyon's walls*

  H *two billion years*

  J *in Earth's history*

5 The picture at the beginning of the selection is intended to —

  A show the route of the Colorado River through the Grand Canyon

  B persuade readers to visit Arizona and see the Grand Canyon

  C point out the rock layers in the sides of the Grand Canyon

  D impress the reader with the size and beauty of the Grand Canyon

STAAR
STATE OF TEXAS ASSESSMENTS OF ACADEMIC READINESS

8.2(A)
Determine the meaning of grade-level academic English words derived from Latin, Greek, or other linguistic roots and affixes.

8.7(A)
Analyze passages in well-known speeches for the author's use of literary devices and word and phrase choice (e.g., aphorisms, epigraphs) to appeal to the audience.

Fig. 19(D)
Make complex inferences about text and use textual evidence to support understanding.

Fig. 19(E)
Summarize, paraphrase, and synthesize texts in ways that maintain meaning and logical order within a text and across texts.

Read the selection and choose the best answer to each question.

from "Advice to Youth"

a speech by Mark Twain (1882)

1   Being told I would be expected to talk here, I inquired what sort of talk I ought to make. They said it should be something suitable to youth—something <u>didactic</u>, instructive, or something in the nature of good advice. Very well. I have a few things in my mind which I have often longed to say for the instruction of the young; for it is in one's tender early years that such things will best take root and be most enduring and most valuable. First, then. I will say to you my young friends—and I say it beseechingly, urgently—

2   Always obey your parents, when they are present. This is the best policy in the long run, because if you don't, they will make you. Most parents think they know better than you do, and you can generally make more by humoring that superstition than you can by acting on your own better judgment.

3   Be respectful to your superiors, if you have any, also to strangers, and sometimes to others. If a person offend you, and you are in doubt as to whether it was intentional or not, do not resort to extreme measures; simply watch your chance and hit him with a brick. That will be sufficient. If you shall find that he had not intended any offense, come out frankly and confess yourself in the wrong when you struck him; acknowledge it like a man and say you didn't mean to. Yes, always avoid violence; in this age of charity and kindliness, the time has gone by for such things. Leave dynamite to the low and unrefined.

4   Go to bed early, get up early—this is wise. Some authorities say get up with the sun; some say get up with one thing, others with another. But a lark is really the best thing to get up with. It gives you a splendid reputation with everybody to know that you get up with the lark; and if you get the right kind of lark, and work at him right, you can easily train him to get up at half past nine, every time—it's no trick at all.

continued ➤

5 Now as to the matter of lying. You want to be very careful about lying; otherwise you are nearly sure to get caught. Once caught, you can never again be in the eyes to the good and the pure, what you were before. Many a young person has injured himself permanently through a single clumsy and ill finished lie, the result of carelessness born of incomplete training. Some authorities hold that the young ought not to lie at all. That, of course, is putting it rather stronger than necessary; still while I cannot go quite so far as that, I do maintain, and I believe I am right, that the young ought to be temperate in the use of this great art until practice and experience shall give them that confidence, elegance, and precision which alone can make the accomplishment graceful and profitable. Patience, diligence, painstaking attention to detail—these are requirements; these in time, will make the student perfect; upon these only, may he rely as the sure foundation for future eminence. Think what tedious years of study, thought, practice, experience, went to the equipment of that peerless old master who was able to impose upon the whole world the lofty and sounding maxim that "Truth is mighty and will prevail"—the most majestic compound fracture of fact which any of woman born has yet achieved. For the history of our race, and each individual's experience, are sewn thick with evidences that a truth is not hard to kill, and that a lie well told is immortal. There is in Boston a monument of the man who discovered anesthesia; many people are aware, in these latter days, that that man didn't discover it at all, but stole the discovery from another man. Is this truth mighty, and will it prevail? Ah no, my hearers, the monument is made of hardy material, but the lie it tells will outlast it a million years. An awkward, feeble, leaky lie is a thing which you ought to make it your unceasing study to avoid; such a lie as that has no more real permanence than an average truth. Why, you might as well tell the truth at once and be done with it. A feeble, stupid, preposterous lie will not live two years—except it be a slander upon somebody. It is indestructible, then of course, but that is no merit of yours. A final word: begin your practice of this gracious and beautiful art early—begin now. If I had begun earlier, I could have learned how.

Name____ Date___________

1 What technique does Twain use to make this speech humorous?

   A He gives common rules for behavior and then twists them in surprising ways.

   B He speaks directly to young people and ignores all of the adults in the audience.

   C He tells an anecdote about a monument in Boston that honors the wrong man.

   D He uses certain well-known words and phrases with new and unusual meanings.

Question 1

Satire is a technique in which the author mocks a subject (such as a person, state, or organization). Satire tends to be humorous. Reread the speech and underline anything you find humorous or satirical.

---

2 Which sentence from the selection best illustrates the technique Twain uses?

   F *Being told I would be expected to talk here, I inquired what sort of talk I ought to make.*

   G *I have a few things in my mind which I have often longed to say for the instruction of the young; for it is in one's tender early years that such things will best take root and be most enduring and most valuable.*

   H *Be respectful to your superiors, if you have any, also to strangers, and sometimes to others.*

   J *Some authorities say get up with the sun; some say get up with one thing, others with another.*

Question 2

Juxtaposition is an element of satire. This happens when the author places two or more things of unequal importance together. This brings everything down to the lowest level of importance.

continued

Name____ Date___________

Question 3

An *aphorism* is a wise saying that contains a general truth. Aphorisms tend to contain humor and sound overworked.

Question 4

Reread the sentences surrounding *didactic* in paragraph 1. *Didactic* comes from the Greek word *didaktikos*, which means "educate or instruct."

Question 5

Think about the tone of a satire. Which answer choice also seems satirical, or humorous? What message is Twain trying to get across to his audience?

3 Which sentence from the selection is an aphorism that Twain uses for effect?

A *This is the best policy in the long run, because if you don't, they will make you.*

B *Most parents think they know better than you do, and you can generally make more by humoring that superstition than you can by acting on your own better judgment.*

C *But a lark is really the best thing to get up with.*

D *Truth is mighty and will prevail.*

---

4 In paragraph 1, the word <u>didactic</u> comes from a Greek root that refers to —

F teaching

G youth

H respect

J lying

---

5 In keeping with the tone of this selection, what is Twain's main message in paragraph 5?

A Young people should be careful not to injure themselves needlessly.

B Truth does not last very long, but a good lie lasts forever.

C Never build a monument for the right person because no one will believe it.

D Elegance, patience, and diligence are the most important traits to develop.

Read the selection and choose the best answer to each question.

STAAR

STATE OF TEXAS ASSESSMENTS OF ACADEMIC READINESS

8.2(B)
Use context (within a sentence and in larger sections of text) to determine or clarify the meaning of unfamiliar or ambiguous words or words with novel meanings.

8.10(B)
Distinguish factual claims from commonplace assertions and opinions and evaluate inferences from their logic in text.

8.10(C)
Make subtle inferences and draw complex conclusions about the ideas in text and their organizational patterns.

8.13(C)
Evaluate various techniques used to create a point of view in media and the impact on audience.

Fig. 19(D)
Make complex inferences about text and use textual evidence to support understanding.

Endurance

1   At the turn of the twentieth century, several European countries were locked in a desperate race to be the first to reach the South Pole—an accomplishment that would be a source of national pride. Ernest Shackleton was one of the British explorers competing to reach the South Pole. He was a gifted sailor and disciplined outdoorsman, but history remembers him mostly as a man who triumphed even in his failures.

2   Shackleton was born on February 15, 1874. He enlisted in the merchant navy when he was sixteen. By 1898, he became a master mariner, meaning he was deemed competent to captain his own vessel. His first attempt at reaching the South Pole ultimately failed, yet it sparked his thirst for adventure.

continued

3   Following another <u>futile</u> bid to claim the South Pole for England in 1907, Shackleton saw his dream collapse. In 1911, a Norwegian named Roald Amundsen became the first man to set foot on the South Pole. Undeterred, Shackleton set out on his third and final journey in 1914. Tragedy struck when his ship, the *Endurance*, became trapped in an ice floe off the coast of Antarctica. After ten months of waiting for help, he and his crew abandoned the sinking ship and survived by hunting penguins and seals on floating ice chunks. With supplies dwindling and the hope of survival fading, Shackleton gathered six of his best sailors on a seven-meter boat called the *James Caird*. He left the majority of the crew behind with little more than a promise to return. After crossing 800 miles of choppy seas in sixteen days, Shackleton reached a whaling station on the island of South Georgia. He returned to pick up his remaining crew on August 30, 1916. Despite impossible odds and treacherous terrain, every member of his crew survived.

Name____ Date___________

1 In paragraph 3, the word <u>futile</u> means —

   A adventurous

   B hopeful

   C contentious

   D unsuccessful

2 Which detail from the selection supports the inference that the trip Shackleton made to the island of South Georgia was dangerous?

   F *off the coast of Antarctica*

   G *After crossing 800 miles of choppy seas*

   H *reached a whaling station*

   J *returned to pick up his remaining crew*

3 What is the author's main argument about Shackleton in this selection?

   A His talent as a sailor allowed him to find success.

   B He was successful at things even when he failed.

   C He was unable to complete his most important missions.

   D His love of adventure caused him to take on dangerous missions.

Question 1

Sometimes, the context clue for a vocabulary word occurs in the sentence or even the paragraph *before* the word. For this question, the last sentence of paragraph 2 provides a context clue.

Question 2

Reread the section of the text that describes Shackleton's trip to South Georgia to check your answer choice.

Question 3

The strongest expression of an author's argument usually occurs at the end of the passage, where authors sum up their points and make the final statement of their claims. Reread the end of the passage to help you answer this question.

continued

Name____ Date___________

Question 4

Facts are thoroughly researched and can be verified through reliable sources such as a historian, encyclopedia, or reference website. Opinions cannot be supported and are more like beliefs.

4 Which sentence from the selection states a fact that can be verified?

F *He was a gifted sailor and disciplined outdoorsman, but history remembers him mostly as a man who triumphed even in his failures.*

G *His first attempt at reaching the South Pole ultimately failed, yet it sparked his thirst for adventure.*

H *Following another futile bid to claim the South Pole for England in 1907, Shackleton saw his dream collapse.*

J *In 1911, a Norwegian named Roald Amundsen became the first man to set foot on the South Pole.*

Question 5

This selection is about the *endurance* of Shackleton and his team. How does the picture at the beginning help illustrate that?

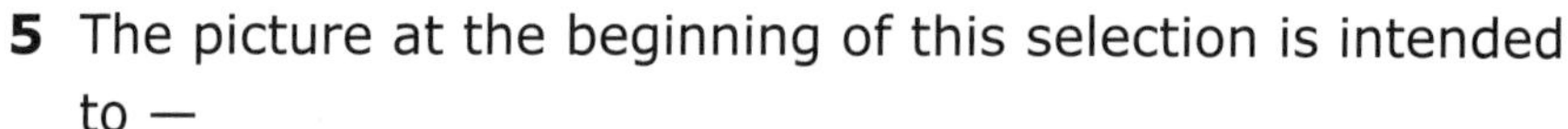

5 The picture at the beginning of this selection is intended to —

A prove that Shackleton reached Antarctica

B show how treacherous the journey was

C explain why Shackleton's mission failed

D identify the location of the *Endurance*

Read the two selections. Then choose the best answer to each question.

from "The Wreck of the Hesperus"

by Henry Wadsworth Longfellow
Source: Project Gutenberg

It was the schooner Hesperus,
    That sailed the wintry sea;
And the skipper had taken his little daughter,
    To bear him company.

5 Blue were her eyes as the fairy-flax,
    Her cheeks like the dawn of day,
And her bosom white as the hawthorn buds,
    That ope in the month of May.

The skipper he stood beside the helm,
10   His pipe was in his mouth,
And he watched how the veering flaw did blow
    The smoke now West, now South.

Then up and spake an old Sailor,
    Had sailed to the Spanish Main,
15 "I pray thee, put into yonder port,
    For I fear a hurricane.

"Last night, the moon had a golden ring,
    And to-night no moon we see!"
The skipper, he blew a whiff from his pipe,
20   And a scornful laugh laughed he.

Colder and louder blew the wind,
    A gale from the Northeast,
The snow fell hissing in the brine,
    And the billows frothed like yeast.

25 Down came the storm, and smote amain
    The vessel in its strength;

continued

She shuddered and paused, like a frighted steed,
    Then leaped her cable's length.

"Come hither! come hither! my little daughter,
30   And do not tremble so;
For I can weather the roughest gale
    That ever wind did blow."

He wrapped her warm in his seaman's coat
    Against the stinging blast;
35 He cut a rope from a broken spar,
    And bound her to the mast.

"O father! I hear the church-bells ring,
    Oh say, what may it be?"
"'Tis a fog-bell on a rock-bound coast!" —
40   And he steered for the open sea.

"O father! I hear the sound of guns,
    Oh say, what may it be?"
"Some ship in distress, that cannot live
    In such an angry sea!"

45 "O father! I see a gleaming light,
    Oh say, what may it be?"
But the father answered never a word,
    A frozen corpse was he.

Lashed to the helm, all stiff and stark,
50   With his face turned to the skies,
The lantern gleamed through the gleaming snow
    On his fixed and glassy eyes.

I Wandered Lonely As a Cloud

by William Wordsworth (1804)
Source: Bartleby.com

I wandered lonely as a cloud
That floats on high o'er vales and hills,
When all at once I saw a crowd,
A host, of golden daffodils;
5 Beside the lake, beneath the trees,
Fluttering and dancing in the breeze.

Continuous as the stars that shine
And twinkle on the milky way,
They stretched in never-ending line
10 Along the margin of a bay:
Ten thousand saw I at a glance,
Tossing their heads in sprightly dance.

The waves beside them danced; but they
Out-did the sparkling waves in glee:
15 A poet could not but be gay,
In such a jocund company:
I gazed—and gazed—but little thought
What wealth the show to me had brought:

For oft, when on my couch I lie
20 In vacant or in pensive mood,
They flash upon that inward eye
Which is the bliss of solitude;
And then my heart with pleasure fills,
And dances with the daffodils.

continued

Name____ Date____________

1 In the selection from "The Wreck of the Hesperus," what makes the old Sailor think a hurricane is coming?

   A He has sailed to the Spanish Main before.

   B He reads the signs in the sky and the moon.

   C He thinks having a woman on board is bad luck.

   D He hears a weather forecast on the radio.

2 In "The Wreck of the Hesperus," the skipper believes that —

   F there is no storm coming

   G the old Sailor is a coward

   H his daughter will bring good luck

   J he can survive any storm

Name____ Date___________

3 Which detail in "The Wreck of the Hesperus" reflects the historical time when the poem was written?

   A The snow falls into the sea.

   B The captain ties his daughter to a mast.

   C The skipper lets his daughter wear his coat.

   D The daughter hears bells ringing in the distance.

---

4 What is the best summary of what happens in this selection from "The Wreck of the Hesperus"?

   F The captain of a ship takes his daughter on a voyage with him. He ignores warnings about a bad storm coming. When the storm hits, the captain ties his daughter to the mast, but the ship is destroyed and he dies.

   G A schooner named *Hesperus* sets off on a voyage during the winter, and the captain's daughter is on board. An old sailor warns that a hurricane is coming and suggests returning to port. The captain refuses to turn around.

   H The captain of a ship sets off on a trip with his daughter tied to the mast. She is wearing his seaman's coat. When a storm strikes, she hears church bells ringing and gunshots. She asks her father what these noises mean.

   J A schooner named *Hesperus* is at sea, and the captain is trying to reach his home port safely. His daughter and an old sailor are members of the crew, but they do not get along with each other. A storm hits and breaks the mast of the ship.

continued

Name____ Date___________

5 In the fourth stanza of "I Wandered Lonely As a Cloud," the daffodils represent a —

   A cloud

   B dance

   C memory

   D friend

---

6 In "I Wandered Lonely As a Cloud," which lines best describe the huge number of daffodils the speaker sees?

   F *When all at once I saw a crowd,*
       A host, of golden daffodils;

   G *Beside the lake, beneath the trees,*
       Fluttering and dancing in the breeze.

   H *Continuous as the stars that shine*
       And twinkle on the milky way

   J *I gazed—and gazed—but little thought*
       What wealth the show to me had brought:

Name____ Date___________

7 The third stanza of "I Wandered Lonely As a Cloud" supports the idea that —

A the speaker enjoyed the waves in the bay more than the daffodils

B seeing the daffodils made the speaker homesick

C the speaker met a poet during his walk in the hills

D seeing the daffodils made the speaker happy

8 What can the reader infer about the speaker in "I Wandered Lonely as a Cloud"?

F He longs for human companionship.

G He is easily impressed by simple things.

H He finds pleasure in his memories.

J He travels to many faraway places.

continued

Name____ Date___________

9 How is the speaker in "I Wandered Lonely As a Cloud" different from the speaker in "The Wreck of the Hesperus"?

   A The speaker in "I Wandered Lonely As a Cloud" describes his own experience; the speaker in "The Wreck of the Hesperus" is an omniscient third-person narrator.

   B The speaker in "I Wandered Lonely As a Cloud" personifies nature; the speaker in "The Wreck of the Hesperus" personifies death.

   C The speaker in "I Wandered Lonely As a Cloud" explains a past memory; the speaker in "The Wreck of the Hesperus" foretells future events.

   D The speaker in "I Wandered Lonely As a Cloud" describes real places and things; the speaker in "The Wreck of the Hesperus" describes events that could not happen.

---

10 How is the purpose of "The Wreck of the Hesperus" different from the purpose of "I Wandered Lonely As a Cloud"?

   F One tells an epic story, and the other describes a moment of enjoying nature.

   G One explains a historical event, and the other explores relationships between people.

   H One describes the power of the sea, and the other emphasizes the bounty of nature.

   J One describes a long journey across the ocean, and the other focuses on walking through a small town.

Read the two selections. Then choose the best answer to each question.

from The "Iron Curtain" Speech

by Winston Churchill (March 5, 1946)

About a year after the end of World War II, Winston Churchill, the former prime minister of Great Britain, gave a speech at a college in Missouri. In his speech, he warned that the world faced two great dangers: war and tyranny. This part of the speech focuses on the dangers of tyranny, especially as practiced by the Soviet Union.

1   Now I come to the second of the two marauders, to the second danger which threatens the cottage home and ordinary people—namely, tyranny. We cannot be blind to the fact that the liberties enjoyed by individual citizens throughout the British Empire are not valid in a considerable number of countries, some of which are very powerful.

2   In these states, control is enforced upon the common people by various kinds of all-embracing police governments, to a degree which is overwhelming and contrary to every principle of democracy. The power of the state is exercised without restraint, either by dictators or by compact oligarchies operating through a privileged party and a political police.

3   It is not our duty at this time, when difficulties are so numerous, to interfere forcibly in the internal affairs of countries which we have not conquered in war. But we must never cease to proclaim in fearless tones the great principles of freedom and the rights of man, which are the joint inheritance of the English-speaking world and which, through Magna Carta, the Bill of Rights, the habeas corpus, trial by jury, and the English common law, find their most famous expression in the American Declaration of Independence.

4   All this means that the people of any country have the right, and should have the power by constitutional action, by free, unfettered elections, with secret ballot, to choose or change the character or form of government under which they dwell; that freedom of speech and thought should reign; that courts of justice, independent of the executive, unbiased by any party, should administer laws which have received the broad assent of large majorities or are <u>consecrated</u> by time and custom. Here are the title deeds of freedom, which should lie in every cottage home. Here is the message of the British and American peoples to mankind. Let us preach what we practise; let us practise what we preach.

continued

from President Ronald Reagan's Address to the British Parliament (1982)

1   We're approaching the end of a bloody century plagued by a terrible political invention—totalitarianism. Optimism comes less easily today, not because democracy is less vigorous, but because democracy's enemies have refined their instruments of repression. Yet optimism is in order, because day by day democracy is proving itself to be a not-at-all-fragile flower. From Stettin on the Baltic to Varna on the Black Sea, the regimes planted by totalitarianism have had more than 30 years to establish their legitimacy. But none—not one regime—has yet been able to risk free elections. Regimes planted by bayonets do not take root.

2   The strength of the Solidarity movement in Poland demonstrates the truth told in an underground joke in the Soviet Union. It is that the Soviet Union would remain a one-party nation even if an opposition party were permitted, because everyone would join the opposition party. [Laughter] . . .

3   Historians looking back at our time will note the consistent restraint and peaceful intentions of the West. They will note that it was the democracies who refused to use the threat of their nuclear monopoly in the forties and early fifties for territorial or imperial gain. Had that nuclear monopoly been in the hands of the Communist world, the map of Europe—indeed, the world—would look very different today. And certainly they will note it was not the democracies that invaded Afghanistan or suppressed Polish Solidarity or used chemical and toxin warfare in Afghanistan and Southeast Asia.

4   If history teaches anything, it teaches self-delusion in the face of unpleasant facts is folly. We see around us today the marks of our terrible dilemma—predictions of doomsday, anti-nuclear demonstrations, an arms race in which the West must, for its own protection, be an unwilling participant. At the same time we see totalitarian forces in the world who seek subversion and conflict around the globe to further their barbarous assault on the human spirit. What, then, is our course? Must civilization perish in a hail of fiery atoms? Must freedom wither in a quiet, deadening accommodation with totalitarian evil?

5   Sir Winston Churchill refused to accept the inevitability of war or even that it was imminent. He said, "I do not believe that Soviet Russia desires war. What they desire is the fruits of war and the indefinite expansion of their power and doctrines. But what we have to consider here today while time remains is the permanent prevention of war and the establishment of conditions of freedom and democracy as rapidly as possible in all countries."

6   Well, this is precisely our mission today: to preserve freedom as well as peace. It may not be easy to see; but I believe we live now at a turning point.

1 In the "Iron Curtain" Speech, Churchill mentions the "danger which threatens cottage home and ordinary people" in paragraph 1 to —

A create an image of freedom and peace in the listener's mind

B appeal to the audience's emotions by instilling fear

C assume that all of his supporters agree with his premise

D describe the possible fate of every democracy

2 According to Churchill's speech, people who live under a "police government" are —

F deprived of basic freedoms enjoyed by others

G unable to work at a job of their choice

H prohibited from holding any public office

J forced to live in government-supplied housing

3 Read this dictionary entry —

> **consecrate** \kon' si krāt\ *verb*
> **1.** to make sacred; dedicate to a deity **2.** to make an object of honor or reverence; establish by tradition **3.** to devote or dedicate to some purpose **4.** to admit or ordain to a religious office or position in a church

Which definition fits the word <u>consecrated</u> in paragraph 4 of Churchill's speech?

A Definition 1

B Definition 2

C Definition 3

D Definition 4

continued

Name____ Date____________

4 Which sentence should be included in a summary of Churchill's speech?

   F Freedom of speech should be a given right for every person.

   G Tyrannical governments violate everyone's right to liberty.

   H The American Declaration of Independence outlines principles of freedom.

   J A nation's laws should be approved by the majority of citizens.

5 In President Reagan's Address to the British Parliament, which statement is based on a false assumption?

   A *Yet optimism is in order, because day by day democracy is proving itself to be a not-at-all-fragile flower.*

   B *The strength of the Solidarity movement in Poland demonstrates the truth told in an underground joke in the Soviet Union.*

   C *Historians looking back at our time will note the consistent restraint and peaceful intentions of the West.*

   D *Sir Winston Churchill refused to accept the inevitability of war or even that it was imminent.*

6 In President Reagan's speech, he quotes Winston Churchill to make the point that —

   F the Soviet Union plans to take over the world by any means necessary

   G everyone has the right to bear arms for self-defense

   H actions committed by tyrannical nations must be condemned

   J democracy can be achieved without going to war

Name____ Date___________

7 In their speeches, both Churchill and Reagan emphasize that people in free nations should be able to —

   A defend their nation through service

   B vote in free and fair elections

   C participate in a trial by jury

   D march in political demonstrations

---

8 Based on these two speeches, Churchill and Reagan would most likely agree with which of these statements?

   F Democratic principles may not work in all nations.

   G Tyranny will ultimately lead to democracy's downfall.

   H It is necessary to remove tyrannical leaders by force.

   J Government by tyranny violates people's civil rights.

continued

Name____ Date____________

9 In these speeches, both Churchill and Reagan conclude that it is important to —

A abide by historical documents

B provide aid to people in other nations

C maintain peaceful relations

D appoint new leaders every few years

---

10 In both of these speeches, the purpose is to —

F promote democracy as the best form of government

G explain why tyranny threatens the entire world

H explain how war with tyrannical nations can be avoided

J dismiss tyranny as a passing phase

Read the next two selections. Then choose the best answer to each question.

The Blacksmith's Helper

1   Jack bolted down the road to the village square, a carpet of brown and gold crunching beneath his feet along the route. It was late September in Philadelphia, and Jack was finished with schooling for the day. With a little apprehension, he hurried to help at the forge, where his father worked as a blacksmith.

2   Tink, tink—Jack heard the sounds of the metal tool shaping the iron as he approached the shop.

3   "I am here, Father!" Jack said in greeting as he dropped his bookbag at the wooden worktable near the wall. He stood respectfully behind his father, waiting until he was acknowledged. Jack's father turned away from the hearth and stepped back to nod and smile at Jack.

4   "Hello, Jackie, my boy! Are you ready to get to work?" His father handed him a leather apron, which Jack obligingly pulled over his head and tied in the back.

continued

5   "I'm ready," Jack answered hesitantly. Although it would be some years before Jack could be an apprentice to his father, he faithfully came to the forge every day to try to be a good helper. His father was good at finding things for Jack to do, like handing him the proper tools or setting out the pieces of iron.

6   Today Jack's father was tasked with fashioning hammerheads and nails for local customers. Jack watched as his father carefully manipulated the hot iron in the fire using a long set of tongs. He was also working on a wheelbarrow. Strong as an ox, his father moved a heavy piece of iron to the anvil and began to pound away with the hammer.

7   Jack moved to the wooden table where he had his own set of tools. He reached for his hammer, wincing at the memory of the thumb he had struck last week with the metal head of a large mallet. He hesitated, thinking maybe he should sweep the floor instead, but Jack's father glanced at him with a knowing look.

8   "Practice makes perfect!" he said with an encouraging smile.

9   Jack bit his lip and reluctantly picked up the hammer, feeling its smooth wooden handle in his hands. He looked over at his father, who was <u>diligently</u> laboring on the wheelbarrow; Jack pushed his insecurities away and began to work.

10   By day's end, Jack had finished his handiwork and revealed his masterpiece to his father.

11   "Unbelievably clever!" exclaimed Jack's father, overlooking the fact that Jack had nailed an old horseshoe to a wooden block, surrounded by tacks that spelled out his name. "I think you'll make a fine blacksmith one day," he said and smiled proudly at his son.

How Moccasins Were Made

1   There once was a beautiful young woman who lived in a small Lenape village with her family. She was known by everyone near and far to be a kind and benevolent young lady. As it happened, there also lived in the village a young man of notable valor who liked the young woman. In addition to his strength and courage, the young man was known across the breadth of the land for his beautiful flute music.

2   One day the young man traversed to the woman's home. Kneeling outside her *wikiyup*, he played an enchanting melody for her on his flute. On hearing the tune, the young woman was charmed by the beautiful music, and she began to like this young man.

3   The young woman soon stepped outside and spoke to the man, explaining to him how she had to walk out of the wikiyup in her bare feet every morning to grind the corn. She earnestly asked if he might think of a way to protect her feet so they wouldn't get dirty when she walked.

4   The young man was very eager to help the young woman and lessen her troublesome burden. He immediately asked his friends to help him prepare a soft piece of deerskin to put on the ground in front of the woman's wikiyup. In this way, she could walk outside to grind corn and not get her feet dirty.

continued

5   The young woman was exceedingly pleased at what the young man had done for her. She then asked if he could keep her feet from getting dirty when she walked to the creek to fetch water. Instantly, the young man once again roused his friends and asked them to help him retrieve more deer hides.

6   Before long, the man's grandfather saw what was happening and forbade his grandson from taking any more of the village's deerskins, for the people would need them for warm clothing and blankets in the cold winter. The young man explained to his grandfather how much he loved the young woman and desperately wanted to do whatever he could to please her. Seeing the young man's wistful countenance, his grandfather conceded to allow just one more skin. He helped the young man make it soft and cut it in the shape of a foot. He cut another skin similarly and gave them both to the young man to give to the young woman.

7   When the young man placed the moccasins on the woman's feet, she was overjoyed: her feet didn't touch the dirty ground! In time, she married the young man, and they lived together happily in the village; and that's how the first moccasins were made.

Name____ Date___________

1 Which sentence from "The Blacksmith's Helper" best shows how Jack is treated by his father?

A *"Are you ready to get to work?"*

B *"Practice makes perfect!" he said with an encouraging smile.*

C *Jack's father turned away from the hearth and stepped back to nod and smile at Jack.*

D *His father was good at finding things for Jack to do, like handing him the proper tools or setting out the pieces of iron.*

2 What is the main conflict in this selection?

F Jack is not sure he can do the job.

G Jack has a lot of schoolwork to do.

H Jack wants to play with his friends.

J Jack and his father do not get along.

3 How is Jack affected by the way his father treats him?

A Jack creates a work that his father overlooks.

B Jack shows that his skills as a blacksmith are as good as his father's.

C Jack finds the confidence to try his best.

D Jack thinks about the times when he has made mistakes.

continued

Name____ Date____________

4 Read this sentence from "The Blacksmith's Helper."

> *Jack bolted down the road to the village square, <u>a carpet of brown and gold</u> crunching beneath his feet along the route.*

Which of the following best explains the meaning of the phrase <u>a carpet of brown and gold</u>?

F the dirt of the unpaved road

G the pattern of bricks lining the route

H the leaves that have fallen from the trees

J the dirty ice and snow covering the ground

5 From "The Blacksmith's Helper," the reader can infer that Jack's father places a high value on —

A using imagination

B healthy living

C trying new things

D hard work

6 In paragraph 9 of "The Blacksmith's Helper," the word <u>diligently</u> means —

F busily

G expertly

H happily

J powerfully

Name____ Date___________

7 In "The Blacksmith's Helper," the narrative point of view helps the reader to —

A compare Jack's work with his father's

B sympathize with Jack's father's concerns

C understand Jack's thoughts and feelings

D visualize the setting of the story

8 How does the grandfather help propel the action of "How Moccasins Were Made"?

F He points out the young man's selfish behavior.

G He encourages the young man to act according to the rules of the village.

H He provides a solution to the young man's problem.

J He helps the young man secretly take the skin from the villagers.

continued

Name____ Date____________

9 Which sentence from the story explains why the grandfather acts as he does?

    A *Before long, the man's grandfather saw what was happening and forbade his grandson from taking any more of the village's deerskins, for the people would need them for warm clothing and blankets in the cold winter.*

    B *The young man was very eager to help the young woman and lessen her troublesome burden.*

    C *The young man explained to his grandfather how much he loved the young woman and desperately wanted to do whatever he could to please her.*

    D *Seeing the young man's wistful countenance, his grandfather conceded to allow just one more skin.*

---

10 What can the reader conclude about the Lenape village in the story "How Moccasins Were Made"?

    F The village is cold all year round.

    G Deerskins are a valuable item in the village.

    H The grandfather makes all of the rules in the village.

    J All of the villagers are charmed by the young man's flute playing.

Name____ Date___________

11 Which of these elements can be found in both "The Blacksmith's Helper" and "How Moccasins Were Made"?

A an older family member who helps by giving support

B a character who hesitates or doubts and then acts

C an explanation that explains the origin of something

D descriptions of a character's inner thoughts

12 Which of these is a theme of both "The Blacksmith's Helper" and "How Moccasins Were Made"?

F Creative people can find unique solutions to problems.

G Children should obey their older family members.

H It is important for people to overcome their feelings of self-doubt if they are to succeed in life.

J Sometimes an individual needs help in order to be successful in creating something meaningful.

13 In "How Moccasins Were Made," why was the young woman first attracted to the young man?

A He knelt on the ground outside her wikiyup.

B He played beautiful music on his flute.

C He put a deer hide on the ground for her.

D He created the first moccasins for her.

continued

Name____ Date___________

14 The illustrations are included with these stories in order to —

   F provide details about the village settings

   G explain why the young men were well liked

   H show what the young men created

   J compare the moccasin to the horseshoe

---

15 What is the best summary of "How Moccasins Were Made"?

   A A beautiful young woman living in a Lenape village walked barefoot all the time and got her feet dirty. A young man who wanted to impress her gave her some moccasins.

   B A young man played his flute for a young woman. She started to like him and asked him to make some moccasins for her. With his grandfather's help, that's what he did.

   C Two young people in a Lenape village needed to find a way to protect their feet as they walked around. They asked their grandfather for help, and he showed the young people how to make moccasins.

   D Long ago, in a Lenape village, a young man wanted to attract a young woman. He played his flute for her and created moccasins out of deer hide to protect her feet. They fell in love and lived happily ever after.

Read the two selections. Then choose the best answer to each question.

Constructing a Monument: Stonehenge

1   More than five thousand years ago, the building of one of the most significant structures in England began. Using primitive tools, quite possibly made from deer antlers, a massive circular ditch and bank called a *henge* was constructed. Archaeologists believe that this marked the early creation of one of the most famous prehistoric sites in Great Britain—Stonehenge.

2   The second phase of Stonehenge continued several centuries later when builders hoisted an estimated eighty bluestones into upright positions. It is believed that the stones were then arranged in either a horseshoe or circular formation.

3   A third phase of construction is estimated to have taken place around 2000 B.C.E. This time, sandstone slabs were arranged into a ring that spanned the outside of the bluestones. Some other sandstone slabs were also assembled into three-piece structures that stand in the center of Stonehenge. Only fifty of these stones remain in place today.

continued

4   One of the great puzzles about Stonehenge is how its early builders managed to transport many of the stones, some of which weighed up to four tons. In analyzing the stones, geologists learned that some of the stones, such as the bluestones, were native to an area in Wales, some two hundred miles away from Stonehenge. They believe that the stones were carried to the site by glaciers. The stones were then deposited in the area of Stonehenge. However, archaeologists are dissatisfied with that theory; they are not convinced that glaciers were entirely responsible for moving the stones. Instead, they have offered up their own theories on how the stones came to Stonehenge. One of these suggests that the builders towed the stones by water on rafts. Then the stones were carried over long, grooved planks with the help of oxen.

5   How the stones arrived at Stonehenge is one mystery—but perhaps an even bigger puzzle is what the purpose of the great monument was. Historians all agree that the structure was clearly noteworthy to its builders, but the function of Stonehenge is still unclear. Some believe that the arrangement of stones signifies a large burial site, while others have suggested that it served as a memorial to honor ancient ancestors or perhaps was used as a special ceremonial site. One astronomer even thought that Stonehenge operated as a kind of calendar. More recently, archaeologists have thought that perhaps the bluestones were considered to have special healing powers for those who were ill.

6   Whatever its purpose, Stonehenge is considered one of the most famous and unique historical sites in the world. Thousands of people come to visit every year, and while the true meaning of Stonehenge may never be entirely understood, its vast stone design will undoubtedly continue to puzzle, intrigue, and prove <u>irresistible</u> to people for many more years.

Sister of Stonehenge

1   Located just twenty miles from the giant stone circles of Stonehenge in England stands what some archaeologists refer to as the "wooden twin" of that famed monument—Woodhenge. The site, like its sister site, is what is called a *henge*, which consists of an earthen bank and ditch.

2   Woodhenge was discovered in 1925 by a pilot flying over the area. The pilot noticed a large pattern of rings; fascinated with his discovery, he reported his finding to a local archaeological society, which then began an excavation of the area. In the process, archaeologists discovered a series of egg-shaped outlines that may have held wooden postholes. In addition to the ditch and the bank, the archaeologists also uncovered a more <u>gruesome</u> find: skeletons of a child and a young man in the ditch. Pottery, chalk tools, and flints were also discovered.

3   Slowly, a picture emerged of what the site might have looked like. There was an entrance on the northeast side of the outlines. The postholes were of varying diameters and depths, which suggested that the posts were of different heights.

continued

4   Scientists believe that Woodhenge dates from 2300 to 2200 B.C.E. This is roughly the same time period as the third phase of construction at Stonehenge. They also have inferred that the site originally consisted of six rings of wooden posts surrounding a central point. Archaeologists also discovered at least five standing stones at the site that may have been part of a separate construction phase, like Stonehenge.

5   But are the two sites truly related? While some people have suggested that Woodhenge was a model for Stonehenge, archaeologists disagree. Given the time period of the Woodhenge site, it appears that Stonehenge and Woodhenge were constructed independently of each other.

6   However, the arrangement of the posts and stones suggests more than a passing similarity to Stonehenge. This similarity has led historians and archaeologists to believe that Woodhenge, like Stonehenge, served as a special spiritual area, such as a site for important ceremonies or a burial ground.

7   Today, decorative cement posts mark the spots where the wood posts once stood. And although Woodhenge may not be as well known as its stone neighbor down the road, and its origins are more obscure, it has no shortage of mystery surrounding it. Although many believe that Stonehenge is a unique site, archaeologists are now asking whether there were more sites similar to Stonehenge and Woodhenge. Together, the two sites offer interesting possibilities about the early history and culture of the peoples of England.

Name____ Date__________

1 In paragraph 6 of "Constructing a Monument: Stonehenge," the word <u>irresistible</u> means —

  A confusing

  B fascinating

  C important

  D mysterious

---

2 The picture in "Constructing a Monument: Stonehenge" is included to —

  F identify the location of Stonehenge

  G describe the source of the bluestones

  H illustrate how Stonehenge worked as a calendar

  J show what Stonehenge looks like

---

3 What can the reader conclude from the information in "Constructing a Monument: Stonehenge"?

  A Different groups of builders worked on Stonehenge's construction.

  B Historians hope to find explanatory documents written by Stonehenge's builders.

  C The climate of Stonehenge has always been the same as it is now.

  D Stonehenge was designed to track the monthly movements of the moon.

continued

Name____ Date___________

4 In "Constructing a Monument: Stonehenge," what are paragraphs 1–3 mainly about?

   F where Stonehenge is located in England

   G what archaeologists think of Stonehenge

   H when and how Stonehenge was built

   J why people in England built Stonehenge

5 Read this sentence from "Constructing a Monument: Stonehenge."

> *One of the great puzzles about Stonehenge is how its early builders managed to transport many of the stones, some of which weighed up to four tons.*

The author uses this sentence in paragraph 4 to introduce information that —

   A is hard to explain

   B might not be accurate

   C scientists do not have evidence for

   D allows only one interpretation

6 Which sentence states a central idea of "Sister of Stonehenge"?

   F Woodhenge, unlike Stonehenge, has been largely rebuilt.

   G Both Woodhenge and Stonehenge were built thousands of years ago.

   H Prehistoric artifacts have been found at both Woodhenge and Stonehenge.

   J Woodhenge, like Stonehenge, is a mysterious site about which we have much to learn.

Name____ Date___________

7 The picture at the beginning of "Sister of Stonehenge" is intended to show —

   A what Woodhenge looked like centuries ago

   B how an airplane pilot first noticed the site

   C a modern interpretation of how the site looked

   D the actual posts still remaining at Woodhenge

8 Read this sentence from "Sister of Stonehenge."

> *In addition to the ditch and the bank, the archaeologists also uncovered a more* gruesome *find: skeletons of a child and a young man in the ditch.*

What does the word gruesome mean as it is used in the sentence?

   F fascinating

   G frightful

   H strange

   J serious

9 What impact does the use of the word gruesome have on the sentence in paragraph 2?

   A It proves to the reader that the monument was used as a burial site.

   B It makes the reader think that the monument is a scary place.

   C It helps the reader appreciate how mysterious the site is.

   D It convinces the reader that building the site was dangerous work.

continued

Name____ Date___________

10 What can the reader conclude about Woodhenge based on "Sister of Stonehenge"?

F Woodhenge was originally used less than Stonehenge was.

G Woodhenge was redesigned by its builders to look more like Stonehenge.

H Evidence of Woodhenge was hidden for thousands of years.

J Evidence of Woodhenge provides many details about prehistoric England.

---

11 Which sentence from "Sister of Stonehenge" supports the idea that Woodhenge and Stonehenge were connected in some way?

A *Woodhenge was discovered in 1925 by a pilot flying over the area.*

B *Archaeologists also discovered at least five standing stones at the site that may have been part of a separate construction phase, like Stonehenge.*

C *While some people have suggested that Woodhenge was a model for Stonehenge, archaeologists disagree.*

D *However, the arrangement of the posts and stones suggests more than a passing similarity to Stonehenge.*

Name____ Date__________

12 Based on the information in both selections, what is one theory that scientists have about both Stonehenge and Woodhenge?

F They were most likely used as a site for burials or important ceremonies.

G They were both constructed in stages over hundreds of years.

H They were both constructed using materials carried from more than 200 miles away.

J They were both used as calendars.

13 In "Sister of Stonehenge," one of the author's main purposes is to —

A persuade people to visit Woodhenge

B explain why Woodhenge was built

C describe the exact location of Woodhenge

D compare Woodhenge to Stonehenge

continued

Name____ Date___________

14 Based on these two selections, what do both Stonehenge and Woodhenge have in common?

F Both were used as altars for religious ceremonies.

G Both were circular constructions built on earthen banks.

H Both were built as calendars for keeping track of time.

J Both were constructed of wooden posts first and then stones.

---

15 On what point do the authors of these selections disagree?

A whether Stonehenge is unique or one of many similar sites

B where Stonehenge is located and what it looks like

C why Woodhenge was built with wooden posts instead of stone slabs

D where the bluestones used at Stonehenge actually came from

Read the two selections. Then choose the best answer to each question.

Prometheus the Fire Giver

1   Long, long ago, the world was ruled by the Titans, led by their king, Kronos. Now Kronos had two sons named Prometheus and Epimetheus. The name Prometheus meant "forethought," and he was always thinking of the future. His brother's name meant "afterthought," and he was always thinking of yesterday.

2   Kronos also had other children, who became the Olympian gods, led by Zeus. But the Titans and the gods did not get along. One day, Kronos challenged Prometheus to create a human being. Kronos wanted someone half as beautiful, intelligent, and powerful as a Titan, but a creature much more advanced than an animal. Basically, he was looking for someone to talk to, someone to teach, and someone who could provide stimulating company.

3   Prometheus, excited by the challenge, sculpted a human from a mound of clay. Humans turned out smart, good, and kind, and Kronos applauded Prometheus on a job well done.

4   Prometheus spent a lot of time teaching people the ways of the world. But after some time, Prometheus saw that they were not doing so well; they were not thriving as they had at the beginning. Men and women were living in caves, shivering from the cold, dying of starvation, and falling victim to wild beasts. Prometheus thought about how he could improve the quality of their lives. After much <u>deliberation</u>, Prometheus realized that fire was the answer. With fire, people would be able to cook food, make tools, and build homes.

5   Unfortunately, while Prometheus was preoccupied with humans, a great battle raged between the Titans and the gods, and the Titans lost. Kronos was exiled forever, so Prometheus had to talk to Zeus about bringing fire to humankind.

6   "Absolutely not!" cried Zeus. "If they had fire, they might become too strong or too wise. After a while, they might drive us out of our own kingdom."

7   Prometheus was not surprised by Zeus's reaction and didn't even bother to respond to it. As he left the king's chambers, he snatched a spark of fire from Zeus's own lightning bolt. Then he showed people how to cook with the fire. They were very happy with this gift; fire made life much easier.

continued

8   But some moons later, Zeus gazed from the mountaintop and caught a glimpse of the fires. He was furious that Prometheus had disobeyed his orders.

9   "Who do you think you are, Prometheus? You do not have the authority to defy my orders!" he shouted.

10   As punishment, Zeus had Prometheus chained to a mountainside. An eagle was ordered to feed every day upon his liver, which would grow back every night. After several generations, Prometheus was freed and allowed to live among humans, his true friends. Even though he was bitterly punished for the gifts that he brought them, he never regretted his actions.

How Maui Brought Fire to the World

1   Long ago in the land of the Maori, a young man named Maui sat beside his fire watching the flames. He thought to himself, "I wonder where fire came from." Being a curious person, Maui decided to find out. That night, while the villagers were sleeping, he traveled to every hut and extinguished every single fire.

2   The next morning, the villagers woke to cold huts and no fire, and they went into a panic. "We can't cook our breakfast," they cried. "We have no way to stay warm. We can't live without fire."

3   Fearful of what would happen to them, the people of the village went to their leader, named Taranga, who was Maui's mother, and asked her what to do. She told them that one of the villagers would have to go and visit her ancestor Mahuika and ask her for fire. None of the villagers was brave enough to risk such a trip, but Maui volunteered to go—after all, Mahuika was his grandmother. Taranga then gave him directions and warned him not to try to trick the fire goddess.

4   Maui left the village and walked for a long time until he reached the entrance to a cave at the base of the fire mountain. Entering the cave, he groped his way through the darkness until suddenly the path opened up into a room filled with fire.

5   "Greetings, Grandson," said a deep and frightening voice from the darkness. "Why do you disturb me in my home?"

6   "The fires of the world have all gone out," said Maui, "and I have come to ask you for fire. The people of the village will not survive without your help."

7   Mahuika listened to Maui's tale and decided to help. She removed one of her burning fingernails and handed it to him. "Take this as a gift, Grandson, and return to your village."

8   So Maui left the cave with the burning fingernail and headed back toward the village. But he had not gotten far when he began to wonder what would happen if Mahuika ran out of fire. So he threw the flaming fingernail into a stream and went back to the cave to ask for another.

continued

9   Mahuika liked her grandson and wanted to help the people, so she gave up another fingernail and sent him on his way. But Maui did the same thing again, and again, and again. Each time, he made up a new excuse and asked for another flame, and each time Mahuika <u>complied</u> by giving him another fingernail, and then a toenail, until finally she had only one left. That's when she realized that Maui had tricked her, and she became enraged.

10   Maui knew he had gone too far. He turned and fled as fast as he could go. Mahuika, furious at being tricked, threw her last toenail at Maui. It missed Maui and landed in the trees. These trees considered fire a great gift and decided to keep it.

11   Barely escaping, Maui continued on to his village. The people were distraught when they realized he had not returned with fire as he had promised. But instead, he brought some dry sticks from the nearby trees and showed the people how to rub them together to form friction. Eventually, the sticks would give up their gift to start a fire.

12   The villagers were happy after that, knowing that they could cook again and stay warm, and now they could make their own fire whenever needed.

Name____ Date___________

1 In paragraph 4 of "Prometheus the Fire Giver," the word <u>deliberation</u> means —

  A anxiety

  B disagreement

  C motivation

  D thought

2 In "Prometheus the Fire Giver," paragraph 4 contributes to the rising action of the story by —

  F revealing the reasons for Kronos's exile

  G presenting the problem Prometheus tries to solve

  H introducing the conflict between Prometheus and Zeus

  J explaining why humans did not live up to Kronos's expectations

3 Based on Prometheus's reaction to Zeus in paragraph 7 of "Prometheus the Fire Giver," what can be inferred about the gods?

  A They were often in conflict with each other.

  B They often abused their power.

  C They were not used to interacting with humans.

  D They caused most of the problems in the world.

continued

Name____ Date___________

4 In "Prometheus the Fire Giver," paragraphs 8 and 9 contribute to the falling action of the story by showing that Zeus is —

   F worried that humans have become too powerful

   G eager to punish other gods

   H angry that Prometheus has disobeyed him

   J unwilling to compromise

---

5 In paragraph 9 of "How Maui Brought Fire to the World," the word <u>complied</u> means —

   A tried to assist

   B met the demand

   C made a sacrifice

   D wondered aloud

---

6 In "How Maui Brought Fire to the World," what is the main problem?

   F The villagers have no fire.

   G No one will visit Mahuika.

   H Maui enrages Mahuika.

   J Maui loses the fire to the trees.

Name____ Date___________

7 In "How Maui Brought Fire to the World," how does Maui's behavior influence the problem?

  A Maui's curiosity enables him to discover a solution to the villagers' problem.

  B Maui's lack of consideration prevents him from helping the villagers.

  C Maui's childish behavior is the cause of the villagers' problem.

  D Maui's close relationship with his grandmother allows him to solve the problem.

8 In "How Maui Brought Fire to the World," how does the rising action help resolve the problem?

  F Maui's long journey reveals the difficulty of the task before him.

  G Taranga's advice helps Maui discover the source of fire and escape with it.

  H The villagers' fear of Mahuika foreshadows the outcome of the story.

  J Taranga makes sure Maui knows that his first obligation is to help the villagers.

continued

Name____ Date____________

9 Which sentence from "How Maui Brought Fire to the World" supports the warning Taranga gives Maui?

   A *"Greetings, Grandson," said a deep and frightening voice from the darkness. "Why do you disturb me in my home?"*

   B *Mahuika liked her grandson and wanted to help the people, so she gave up another fingernail and sent him on his way.*

   C *Each time, he made up a new excuse and asked for another flame, and each time Mahuika complied by giving him another fingernail, and then a toenail, until finally she had only one left.*

   D *That's when she realized that Maui had tricked her, and she became enraged.*

10 The trees in "How Maui Brought Fire to the World" are significant because they —

   F show Maui how fire first originated

   G enable Maui to make his own fire

   H save Maui from Mahuika's rage

   J provide shelter for the villagers

11 The purpose in both of these selections is to —

   A explore the relationships among the deities

   B explain where fire originally came from

   C describe the hardships of life in ancient times

   D explain where humans originally came from

Name____ Date____________

12 Which is an accurate comparison of Maui and Prometheus in these two selections?

F Both characters are sent on quests, but Prometheus's quest is unreasonable and Maui's is attainable.

G Both characters disobey the advice they get, but Prometheus feels regretful and Maui does not.

H Prometheus is embraced by humankind, but Maui is shunned by the villagers.

J Prometheus feels morally obligated to help humans, but Maui acts only for his personal satisfaction.

13 Which of these elements Is found in both myths?

A The deities overstep their authority.

B The main character responds to a challenge.

C Nature causes a problem for humans.

D Relationships among family members are tested.

continued

Name____ Date____________

14 In these two selections, both Zeus and Mahuika are —

F helpful

G unreasonable

H vengeful

J sympathetic

---

15 Which thematic element is apparent in both myths?

A the importance of fire

B the existence of an afterlife

C the value of listening to elders

D the cruelty of nature

Warm-Up 1 • from *Heidi*

Question & Answer	Standard
1 Read this sentence from the excerpt from *Heidi*. *The youngster's cheeks were <u>in such a glow</u> that it showed even through her sun-browned skin.* What is the meaning of <u>in such a glow</u> as it is used in this sentence? **A red** B shiny C pale D sweaty	8.2(B)
2 In this selection, the narrator is — F the girl named Deta G an unnamed villager H third-person limited **J third-person omniscient**	8.6(C)
3 Which sentence from the excerpt supports the inference that Alm is a small town and everyone knows each other? A *One bright sunny morning in June, a tall, vigorous maiden of the mountain region climbed up the narrow path, leading a little girl by the hand.* B *Her shape was difficult to distinguish, for she wore two dresses, if not three, and around her shoulders a large red cotton shawl.* C The pair had been climbing for about an hour when they reached a hamlet half-way up the great mountain named the Alm. **D *It was the elder girl's home town, and therefore she was greeted from nearly every house; people called to her from windows and doors, and very often from the road.***	8.6 Fig. 19(D)
4 How does Deta plan to resolve the conflict in this excerpt? F She and the girl will go back down the mountain. **G She is going to leave the girl with her grandfather.** H She plans to send the girl away to a boarding school. J She will find a new home for the girl in the village.	8.6(A)

Warm-Up 2 • Weather Patterns

Question & Answer	Standard
1 Read the dictionary entry. wave \wāv\ *noun* **1.** a moving ridge or swell of water on a sea or lake **2.** a widespread movement of people or animals **3.** a greeting made with the hand **4.** a period of unusually hot or cold weather Which definition of <u>wave</u> is used in paragraph 1? A Definition 1 B Definition 2 C Definition 3 **D Definition 4**	**8.2(E)**
2 Based on the information in this selection, the reader can conclude that — F air masses form only over land **G understanding jet streams can help people predict local weather** H jet streams form only in the United States J each of Earth's oceans causes different weather patterns	**8.10(C)**
3 What is paragraph 2 mainly about? A Air masses are carried around the country by jet streams. B In 2011, it was above 100°F for 52 days in a row in Wichita Falls, Texas. **C Jet streams are strong winds caused by temperature differences between air masses.** D Small temperature differences between air masses lead to longer weather patterns.	**8.10(A)**
4 The diagram is included in this selection to — F describe the cause of storms in the United States **G illustrate the flow of the jet streams** H show the location of La Niña in the Pacific Ocean J explain the differences in air temperatures	**8.13(A)**

Answer Key

Warm-Up 3 • from *The Post Office*

Question & Answer	Standard
1 In this play, what can the reader learn from the stage directions at the beginning? A where Amal goes to school B why the Physician has left C what Madhav does for work **D why Amal cannot go outside**	**8.5 Fig. 19(D)**
2 Which line from the play reveals Madhav's view of education? F Doctor says it's bad for you to be out. G What a thing to say! The doctor can't know and he reads such huge books! **H *Dear, dear; it would have been my saving if I could have been learned.*** J Else, what was the use in heaping up so many large stones to make such a big affair of it, eh!	**8.5(A)**
3 Which detail in the play shows that Madhav and Amal see things differently? **A Madhav sees the mountain as a barrier, but Amal sees it as an invitation.** B Madhav sees Amal's illness as a weakness, but Amal sees it as a strength. C Madhav sees work as an exciting opportunity, but Amal sees it as a burden. D Madhav sees the doctor as a fraud, but Amal sees him as an authority.	**8.5(A)**
4 How does the society he lives in affect Madhav's views? F He does not think the doctor has enough experience to diagnose illness. **G He believes it is very important for Amal to become learned.** H He wants Amal to leave home soon and experience different parts of the world. J He thinks that Auntie, not his uncle, should take care of Amal.	**8.3(C)**

Warm-Up 4 • The Bone Wars

Question & Answer	Standard
1 Which sentence expresses a main idea of "The Bone Wars"? A Competition between scientists in a field of study leads to handsome rewards. B Scientific rivals encourage each other to do their best work. **C The rivalry between both Marsh and Cope had both positive and negative results.** D Colorado holds the most important dinosaur fossils found.	**8.10(A)**
2 Which detail from the selection supports the idea that Marsh and Cope would do anything to win the competition between them? **F *They even had their workers deliberately destroy fossils so the other man could not collect them.*** G *The contest between the two climaxed in 1877 with the discovery of fossils at two separate sites in Colorado.* H *. . . it is believed that more than 142 new species were discovered as a result of their work.* J *It would appear that Marsh won the Bone Wars with his discovery of some eighty new dinosaur fossils.*	**8.10 Fig. 19(D)**
3 Which sentence from the selection states a fact? A *One of the longest and most bitter rivalries in nineteenth-century America was not over gold, timber, or coal–but over dinosaur bones.* B *For over twenty years, the two men engaged in a competition that was as bitter as it was fierce.* C *For both Marsh and Cope, there were no measures too extreme or too outrageous in the race to become the reigning dinosaur hunter.* **D *Marsh would eventually uncover the first known remains of the dinosaurs* Stegosaurus *and* Brontosaurus.**	**8.10(B)**
4 In paragraph 5, the word <u>galvanized</u> means – F reduced; lessened **G stimulated; stirred** H dulled; dampened J ridiculed; laughed at	**8.2(A)**

Answer Key

STAAR Reading Warm-Ups & Test Practice Grade 8 • ©2014 Newmark Learning, LLC

Warm-Up 5 • An Unexpected Treasure

Question & Answer	Standard
1 The conflict in this story is resolved when Juan – **A finds a license plate buried in the sand** B decides to leave home and become a pirate C becomes frustrated with the hunt along the beach D learns how to work the metal detector at the end of the day	**8.6(A)**
2 In paragraph 2 of the story, the word <u>combing</u> means – F tidying **G searching** H raking J digging	**8.2(B)**
3 Juan finally finds something at the end of the day because he is – A creative and enthusiastic **B patient and determined** C curious and imaginative D angry and frustrated	**8.6(B)**
4 Which sentence from the story supports the inference that Juan's wife understands his obsession? F *As the years marched on, Juan became taller and wiser, yet he never outgrew his obsession.* **G *One sunny day, his wife presented him with a state-of-the-art metal detector and smiled broadly as Juan excitedly bounded out the door with it.*** H *Juan strolled along the beach, running the end of his device over miles of sugar-white sand as hours passed by and the sun began its descent into the sea.* J *With fingers trembling, Juan ran the disk of his metal detector back over the spot, straining his ears to hear the digital alarm sound out again.*	**8.6 Fig. 19(D)**

Warm-Up 6 • How to Fix a Flat Bike Tire

Question & Answer	Standard
1 Based on this selection, the reader can infer that a tire repair kit includes – A a spare tube B a set of wrenches **C glue and a patch** D new brake pads	**8.12 Fig. 19(D)**
2 What might be on a person's bike that is not shown in the first picture in this selection? F tire G rim H brake pads **J axle nut**	**8.12(B)**
3 The picture next to Step 3 is included to show how to – A find the leak **B use a tire lever** C patch the hole D remove the tube	**8.12(B)**
4 When repairing a flat bike tire, a pail of water is useful for – F washing the tire G rinsing the brake pads **H locating the leak** J cleaning one's hands	**8.12 Fig. 19(D)**
5 Read the dictionary entry. **instrument** \in' strə mənt\ *noun* **1.** a mechanical tool or implement **2.** a device for producing musical sounds **3.** a device for measuring quantity or amount **4.** an agent or agency by which something is done, as in government programs Which definition fits the word <u>instrument</u> in Step 3 of the selection? **A Definition 1** B Definition 2 C Definition 3 D Definition 4	**8.2(E)**

Warm-Up 7 • from *The Adventures of Tom Sawyer*

Question & Answer	Standard
1 In this selection, the author included paragraph 2 in order to — A explain why Tom's enthusiasm for painting quickly faded away B show the reader that Tom has no money or valuables C reveal that Tom knows a lot of boys but has no real friends **D let the reader know that Tom wants to get out of his situation**	**8.6(A)**
2 The reader can conclude that when Tom sees Ben Rogers approaching, Tom feels — F amused **G apprehensive** H relieved J surprised	**8.6(B)**
3 In paragraph 1, the phrase <u>burnt him like fire</u> suggests that Tom was — **A resentful** B satisfied C exhausted D sunburned	**8.8(A)**
4 The narrative point of view in this story enables the reader to — F predict what Ben Rogers will do next G figure out that Tom Sawyer is an orphan H identify the details of the setting **J understand Tom's thoughts and feelings**	**8.6(C)**
5 Which of the characters' actions in this story is influenced by the setting? A Tom finds pieces of toys and trash in his pocket. B Tom decides to find someone else to do his work. **C Ben Rogers pretends to be on a steamboat on the river.** D Ben Rogers walks down the street eating a snack.	**8.3(C)**

Warm-Up 8 • The Storytelling Canyon

Question & Answer	Standard
1 Which sentence expresses a main idea of this selection? A The Grand Canyon is a popular tourist destination. **B The Grand Canyon reveals much about Earth's history.** C Many artifacts can be found in the rocks of the Grand Canyon. D The Colorado River formed the Grand Canyon over millions of years.	**8.10(A)**
2 How is the central idea developed over the course of the selection? F Each successive paragraph gives details from further back in Earth's history. G Each successive paragraph gives a different reason why people visit the canyon. H First the history of the canyon is described, and then the reasons why people visit the canyon are listed. **J First the formation of the canyon is described, and then the kind of evidence found in the canyon is outlined.**	**8.10(C)**
3 What connection does "The Storytelling Canyon" make between the size of the Grand Canyon and its usefulness to scientists? A The depth of the canyon allows scientists to study the effects of water erosion on the land. **B The depth of the canyon allows scientists to learn about distant periods in the history of Earth.** C The length and width of the canyon allow scientists to examine many different types and colors of soil. D The length and width of the canyon allow scientists to study a large section of the surface of Earth.	**8.10(D)**
4 Which phrase in paragraph 3 helps the reader understand the meaning of the word <u>strata</u>? **F *rock layers*** G *canyon's walls* H *two billion years* J *in Earth's history*	**8.2(A)**
5 The picture at the beginning of the selection is intended to – A show the route of the Colorado River through the Grand Canyon B persuade readers to visit Arizona and see the Grand Canyon C point out the rock layers in the sides of the Grand Canyon **D impress the reader with the size and beauty of the Grand Canyon**	**8.13(C)**

Answer Key

STAAR Reading Warm-Ups & Test Practice Grade 8 • ©2014 Newmark Learning, LLC

Warm-Up 9 • from "Advice to Youth"

Question & Answer	Standard
1 What technique does Twain use to make this speech humorous? **A He gives common rules for behavior and then twists them in surprising ways.** B He speaks directly to young people and ignores all of the adults in the audience. C He tells an anecdote about a monument in Boston that honors the wrong man. D He uses certain well-known words and phrases with new and unusual meanings.	**8.7(A)**
2 Which sentence from the selection best illustrates the technique Twain uses? F *Being told I would be expected to talk here, I inquired what sort of talk I ought to make.* G *I have a few things in my mind which I have often longed to say for the instruction of the young; for it is in one's tender early years that such things will best take root and be most enduring and most valuable.* **H *Be respectful to your superiors, if you have any, also to strangers, and sometimes to others.*** J *Some authorities say get up with the sun; some say get up with one thing, others with another.*	**8.7 Fig. 19(D)**
3 Which sentence from the selection is an aphorism that Twain uses for effect? A *This is the best policy in the long run, because if you don't, they will make you.* B *Most parents think they know better than you do, and you can generally make more by humoring that superstition than you can by acting on your own better judgment.* C *But a lark is really the best thing to get up with.* **D *Truth is mighty and will prevail.***	**8.7(A)**
4 In paragraph 1, the word <u>didactic</u> comes from a Greek root that refers to — **F teaching** G youth H respect J lying	**8.2(A)**
5 In keeping with the tone of this selection, what is Twain's main message in paragraph 5? A Young people should be careful not to injure themselves needlessly. **B Truth does not last very long, but a good lie lasts forever.** C Never build a monument for the right person because no one will believe it. D Elegance, patience, and diligence are the most important traits to develop.	**8.7 Fig. 19(E)**

Warm-Up 10 • Endurance

Question & Answer	Standard
1 In paragraph 3, the word <u>futile</u> means – A adventurous B hopeful C controversial **D unsuccessful**	**8.2(B)**
2 Which detail from the selection supports the inference that the trip Shackleton made to the island of South Georgia was dangerous? F *off the coast of Antarctica* **G *After crossing 800 miles of choppy seas*** H *reached a whaling station* J *returned to pick up his remaining crew*	**8.10 Fig. 19(D)**
3 What is the author's main argument about Shackleton in this selection? A His talent as a sailor allowed him to find success. **B He was successful at things even when he failed.** C He was unable to complete his most important missions. D His love of adventure caused him to take on dangerous missions.	**8.10(C)**
4 Which sentence from the selection states a fact that can be verified? F *He was a gifted sailor and disciplined outdoorsman, but history remembers him mostly as a man who triumphed even in his failures.* G *His first attempt at reaching the South Pole ultimately failed, yet it sparked his thirst for adventure.* H *Following another futile bid to claim the South Pole for England in 1907, Shackleton saw his dream collapse.* **J *In 1911, a Norwegian named Roald Amundsen became the first man to set foot on the South Pole.***	**8.10(B)**
5 The picture at the beginning of this selection is intended to – A prove that Shackleton reached Antarctica **B show how treacherous the journey was** C explain why Shackleton's mission failed D identify the location of the *Endurance*	**8.13(C)**

Practice Test 1 • from "The Wreck of the Hesperus" • "I Wandered Lonely As a Cloud"

Question & Answer	Standard
1 In the selection from "The Wreck of the Hesperus," what makes the old Sailor think a hurricane is coming? A He has sailed to the Spanish Main before. **B He reads the signs in the sky and the moon.** C He thinks having a woman on board is bad luck. D He hears a weather forecast on the radio.	**8.3(C)**
2 In "The Wreck of the Hesperus," the skipper believes that – F there is no storm coming G the old Sailor is a coward H his daughter will bring good luck **J he can survive any storm**	**8.3 Fig. 19(D)**
3 Which detail in "The Wreck of the Hesperus" reflects the historical time when the poem was written? A The snow falls into the sea. **B The captain ties his daughter to a mast.** C The skipper lets his daughter wear his coat. D The daughter hears bells ringing in the distance.	**8.3(C)**

Question & Answer	Standard
4 What is the best summary of what happens in this selection from "The Wreck of the Hesperus"? **F The captain of a ship takes his daughter on a voyage with him. He ignores warnings about a bad storm coming. When the storm hits, the captain ties his daughter to the mast, but the ship is destroyed and he dies.** G A schooner named Hesperus sets off on a voyage during the winter, and the captain's daughter is on board. An old sailor warns that a hurricane is coming and suggests returning to port. The captain refuses to turn around. H The captain of a ship sets off on a trip with his daughter tied to the mast. She is wearing his seaman's coat. When a storm strikes, she hears church bells ringing and gun shots. She asks her father what these noises mean. J A schooner named Hesperus is at sea, and the captain is trying to reach his home port safely. His daughter and an old sailor are members of the crew, but they do not get along with each other. A storm hits and breaks the mast of the ship.	**8.4 Fig. 19(E)**
5 In the fourth stanza of "I Wandered Lonely As a Cloud," the daffodils represent a — A cloud B dance **C memory** D friend	**8.8(A)**
6 In "I Wandered Lonely As a Cloud," which lines best describe the huge number of daffodils the speaker sees? F *When all at once I saw a crowd,* *A host, of golden daffodils;* G *Beside the lake, beneath the trees,* *Fluttering and dancing in the breeze.* **H Continuous as the stars that shine** **And twinkle on the milky way** J *I gazed–and gazed–but little thought* *What wealth the show to me had brought:*	**8.8(A)**

Question & Answer	Standard
7 The third stanza of "I Wandered Lonely As a Cloud" supports the idea that – A the speaker enjoyed the waves in the bay more than the daffodils B seeing the daffodils made the speaker homesick C the speaker met a poet during his walk in the hills **D seeing the daffodils made the speaker happy**	**8.4 Fig. 19(D)**
8 What can the reader infer about the speaker in "I Wandered Lonely as a Cloud"? F He longs for human companionship. G He is easily impressed by simple things. **H He finds pleasure in his memories.** J He travels to many faraway places.	**8.4 Fig. 19(D)**
9 How is the speaker in "I Wandered Lonely As a Cloud" different from the speaker in "The Wreck of the Hesperus"? **A The speaker in "I Wandered Lonely As a Cloud" describes his own experience; the speaker in "The Wreck of the Hesperus" is an omniscient third-person narrator.** B The speaker in "I Wandered Lonely As a Cloud" personifies nature; the speaker in "The Wreck of the Hesperus" personifies death. C The speaker in "I Wandered Lonely As a Cloud" explains a past memory; the speaker in "The Wreck of the Hesperus" foretells future events. D The speaker in "I Wandered Lonely As a Cloud" describes real places and things; the speaker in "The Wreck of the Hesperus" describes events that could not happen.	**8.4(A)**
10 How is the purpose of "The Wreck of the Hesperus" different from the purpose of "I Wandered Lonely As a Cloud"? **F One tells an epic story, and the other describes a moment of enjoying nature.** G One explains a historical event, and the other explores relationships between people. H One describes the power of the sea, and the other emphasizes the bounty of nature. J One describes a long journey across the ocean, and the other focuses on walking through a small town.	**8.4(A)**

Practice Test 2 • from the "Iron Curtain" Speech • from President Reagan's Address

Question & Answer	Standard
1 In the "Iron Curtain" Speech, Churchill mentions the "danger which threatens cottage home and ordinary people" in paragraph 1 to — A create an image of freedom and peace in the listener's mind **B appeal to the audience's emotions by instilling fear** C assume that all of his supporters agree with his premise D describe the possible fate of every democracy	**8.11(B)**
2 According to Churchill's speech, people who live under a "police government" are — **F deprived of basic freedoms enjoyed by others** G unable to work at a job of their choice H prohibited from holding any public office J forced to live in government-supplied housing	**8.11 Fig. 19(D)**
3 Read this dictionary entry. **consecrate** \kon' si krāt\ *verb* **1.** to make sacred; dedicate to a deity **2.** to make an object of honor or reverence; establish by tradition **3.** to devote or dedicate to some purpose **4.** to admit or ordain to a religious office or position in a church Which definition fits the word <u>consecrated</u> in paragraph 4 of Churchill's speech? A Definition 1 **B Definition 2** C Definition 3 D Definition 4	**8.2(E)**
4 Which sentence should be included in a summary of Churchill's speech? F Freedom of speech should be a given right for every person. **G Tyrannical governments violate everyone's right to liberty.** H The American Declaration of Independence outlines principles of freedom. J A nation's laws should be approved by the majority of citizens.	**8.11 Fig. 19(E)**
5 In President Reagan's Address to the British Parliament, which statement is based on a false assumption? A *Yet optimism is in order, because day by day democracy is proving itself to be a not-at-all-fragile flower.* B *The strength of the Solidarity movement in Poland demonstrates the truth told in an underground joke in the Soviet Union.* **C *Historians looking back at our time will note the consistent restraint and peaceful intentions of the West.*** D *Sir Winston Churchill refused to accept the inevitability of war or even that it was imminent.*	**8.11(B)**

Question & Answer	Standard
6 In President Reagan's speech, he quotes Winston Churchill to make the point that – F the Soviet Union plans to take over the world by any means necessary G everyone has the right to bear arms for self-defense H actions committed by tyrannical nations must be condemned **J** **democracy can be achieved without going to war**	**8.11 Fig. 19(D)**
7 In their speeches, both Churchill and Reagan emphasize that people in free nations should be able to – A defend their nation through service **B** **vote in free and fair elections** C participate in a trial by jury D march in political demonstrations	**8.11(A)**
8 Based on these two speeches, Churchill and Reagan would most likely agree with which of these statements? F Democratic principles may not work in all nations. G Tyranny will ultimately lead to democracy's downfall. H It is necessary to remove tyrannical leaders by force. **J** **Government by tyranny violates people's civil rights.**	**8.11 Fig. 19(F)**
9 In these speeches, both Churchill and Reagan conclude that it is important to – A abide by historical documents B provide aid to people in other nations **C** **maintain peaceful relations** D appoint new leaders every few years	**8.11(A)**
10 In both of these speeches, the purpose is to – **F** **promote democracy as the best form of government** G explain why tyranny threatens the entire world H explain how war with tyrannical nations can be avoided J dismiss tyranny as a passing phase	**8.9(A)**

Practice Test 3 • The Blacksmith's Helper • How Moccasins Were Made

Question & Answer	Standard
1 Which sentence from "The Blacksmith's Helper" best shows how Jack is treated by his father? A "Are you ready to get to work?" **B "Practice makes perfect!" he said with an encouraging smile.** C Jack's father turned away from the hearth and stepped back to nod and smile at Jack. D His father was good at finding things for Jack to do, like handing him the proper tools or setting out the pieces of iron.	**8.6 Fig. 19(D)**
2 What is the main conflict in this selection? **F Jack is not sure he can do the job.** G Jack has a lot of schoolwork to do. H Jack wants to play with his friends. J Jack and his father do not get along.	**8.6(A)**
3 How is Jack affected by the way his father treats him? A Jack creates a work that his father overlooks. B Jack shows that his skills as a blacksmith are as good as his father's. **C Jack finds the confidence to try his best.** D Jack thinks about the times when he has made mistakes.	**8.6(B)**
4 Read this sentence from "The Blacksmith's Helper." Jack bolted down the road to the village square, a <u>carpet of brown and gold</u> crunching beneath his feet along the route. Which of the following best explains the meaning of the phrase a <u>carpet of brown and gold</u>? F the dirt of the unpaved road G the pattern of bricks lining the route **H the leaves that have fallen from the trees** J the dirty ice and snow covering the ground	**8.8(A)**

Question & Answer	Standard
5 From "The Blacksmith's Helper," the reader can infer that Jack's father places a high value on— A using imagination B healthy living C trying new things **D hard work**	**8.3(A)**
6 In paragraph 9 of "The Blacksmith's Helper," the word <u>diligently</u> means— **F busily** G expertly H happily J powerfully	**8.2(B)**
7 In "The Blacksmith's Helper," the narrative point of view helps the reader to— A compare Jack's work with his father's B sympathize with Jack's father's concerns **C understand Jack's thoughts and feelings** D visualize the setting of the story	**8.6(C)**
8 How does the grandfather help propel the action of "How Moccasins Were Made"? F He points out the young man's selfish behavior. G He encourages the young man to act according to the rules of the village. **H He provides a solution to the young man's problem.** J He helps the young man secretly take the skin from the villagers.	**8.6(A)**

Question & Answer	Standard
9 Which sentence from the story explains why the grandfather acts as he does? A *Before long, the man's grandfather saw what was happening and forbade his grandson from taking any more of the village's deerskins, for the people would need them for warm clothing and blankets in the cold winter.* B *The young man was very eager to help the young woman and lessen her troublesome burden.* C *The young man explained to his grandfather how much he loved the young woman and desperately wanted to do whatever he could to please her.* **D *Seeing the young man's wistful countenance, his grandfather conceded to allow just one more skin.***	8.6(B)
10 What can the reader conclude about the Lenape village in the story "How Moccasins Were Made"? F The village is cold all year round. **G Deerskins are a valuable item in the village.** H The grandfather makes all of the rules in the village. J All of the villagers are charmed by the young man's flute playing.	8.3(C)
11 Which of these elements can be found in both "The Blacksmith's Helper" and "How Moccasins Were Made"? **A an older family member who helps by giving support** B a character who hesitates or doubts and then acts C an explanation that explains the origin of something D descriptions of a character's inner thoughts	8.6 Fig. 19(F)
12 Which of these is a theme of both "The Blacksmith's Helper" and "How Moccasins Were Made"? F Creative people can find unique solutions to problems. G Children should obey their older family members. H It is important for people to overcome their feelings of self-doubt if they are to succeed in life. **J Sometimes an individual needs help in order to be successful in creating something meaningful.**	8.3(A)

STAAR Reading Warm-Ups & Test Practice Grade 8 • ©2014 Newmark Learning, LLC

Question & Answer	Standard
13 In "How Moccasins Were Made," why was the young woman first attracted to the young man? A He knelt on the ground outside her wikiyup. **B He played beautiful music on his flute.** C He put a deer hide on the ground for her. D He created the first moccasins for her.	**8.6(A)**
14 The illustrations are included with these stories in order to – F provide details about the village settings G explain why the young men were well liked **H show what the young men created** J compare the moccasin to the horseshoe	**8.13(A)**
15 What is the best summary of "How Moccasins Were Made"? A A beautiful young woman living in a Lenape village walked barefoot all the time and got her feet dirty. A young man who wanted to impress her gave her some moccasins. B A young man played his flute for a young woman. She started to like him and asked him to make some moccasins for her. With his grandfather's help, that's what he did. C Two young people in a Lenape village needed to find a way to protect their feet as they walked around. They asked their grandfather for help, and he showed the young people how to make moccasins. **D Long ago, in a Lenape village, a young man wanted to attract a young woman. He played his flute for her and created moccasins out of deer hide to protect her feet. They fell in love and lived happily ever after.**	**8.10(A)**

Practice Test 4 • Constructing a Monument: Stonehenge Sister of Stonehenge

Question & Answer	Standard
1 In paragraph 6 of "Constructing a Monument: Stonehenge," the word <u>irresistible</u> means – A confusing **B fascinating** C important D mysterious	**8.2(A)**
2 The picture in "Constructing a Monument: Stonehenge" is included to – F identify the location of Stonehenge G describe the source of the bluestones H illustrate how Stonehenge worked as a calendar **J show what Stonehenge looks like**	**8.13(A)**
3 What can the reader conclude from the information in "Constructing a Monument: Stonehenge"? **A Different groups of builders worked on Stonehenge's construction.** B Historians hope to find explanatory documents written by Stonehenge's builders. C The climate of Stonehenge has always been the same as it is now. D Stonehenge was designed to track the monthly movements of the moon.	**8.10(C)**
4 In "Constructing a Monument: Stonehenge," what are paragraphs 1–3 mainly about? F where Stonehenge is located in England G what archaeologists think of Stonehenge **H when and how Stonehenge was built** J why people in England built Stonehenge	**8.10(A)**

Question & Answer	Standard
5 Read this sentence from "Constructing a Monument: Stonehenge." *One of the great puzzles about Stonehenge is how its early builders managed to transport many of the stones, some of which weighed up to four tons.* The author uses this sentence in paragraph 4 to introduce information that – **A is hard to explain** B might not be accurate C scientists do not have evidence for D allows only one interpretation	**8.10(C)**
6 Which sentence states a central idea of "Sister of Stonehenge"? F Woodhenge, unlike Stonehenge, has been largely rebuilt. G Both Woodhenge and Stonehenge were built thousands of years ago. H Prehistoric artifacts have been found at both Woodhenge and Stonehenge. **J Woodhenge, like Stonehenge, is a mysterious site about which we have much to learn.**	**8.10(A)**
7 The picture at the beginning of "Sister of Stonehenge" is intended to show – A what Woodhenge looked like centuries ago B how an airplane pilot first noticed the site **C a modern interpretation of how the site looked** D the actual posts still remaining at Woodhenge	**8.13(C)**
8 Read this sentence from "Sister of Stonehenge." *In addition to the ditch and the bank, the archaeologists also uncovered a more gruesome find: skeletons of a child and a young man in the ditch.* What does the word gruesome mean as it is used in the sentence? F fascinating **G frightful** H strange J serious	**8.2(B)**

Question & Answer	Standard
9 What impact does the use of the word <u>gruesome</u> have on the sentence in paragraph 2? A It proves to the reader that the monument was used as a burial site. B It makes the reader think that the monument is a scary place. **C It helps the reader appreciate how mysterious the site is.** D It convinces the reader that building the site was dangerous work.	**8.2(B)**
10 What can the reader conclude about Woodhenge based on "Sister of Stonehenge"? F Woodhenge was originally used less than Stonehenge was. G Woodhenge was redesigned by its builders to look more like Stonehenge. **H Evidence of Woodhenge was hidden for thousands of years.** J Evidence of Woodhenge provides many details about prehistoric England.	**8.10(D)**
11 Which sentence from "Sister of Stonehenge" supports the idea that Woodhenge and Stonehenge were connected in some way? A Woodhenge was discovered in 1925 by a pilot flying over the area. B *Archaeologists also discovered at least five standing stones at the site that may have been part of a separate construction phase, like Stonehenge.* C *While some people have suggested that Woodhenge was a model for Stonehenge, archaeologists disagree.* **D *However, the arrangement of the posts and stones suggests more than a passing similarity to Stonehenge.***	**8.10 Fig. 19(D)**
12 Based on the information in both selections, what is one theory that scientists have about both Stonehenge and Woodhenge? **F They were most likely used as a site for burials or important ceremonies.** G They were both constructed in stages over hundreds of years. H They were both constructed using materials carried from more than 200 miles away. J They were both used as calendars.	**8.10 Fig. 19(F)**

Question & Answer	Standard
13 In "Sister of Stonehenge," one of the author's main purposes is to – A persuade people to visit Woodhenge B explain why Woodhenge was built C describe the exact location of Woodhenge **D compare Woodhenge to Stonehenge**	**8.9(A)**
14 Based on these two selections, what do both Stonehenge and Woodhenge have in common? F Both were used as altars for religious ceremonies. **G Both were circular constructions built on earthen banks.** H Both were built as calendars for keeping track of time. J Both were constructed of wooden posts first and then stones.	**8.10 Fig. 19(F)**
15 On what point do the authors of these selections disagree? **A whether Stonehenge is unique or one of many similar sites** B where Stonehenge is located and what it looks like C why Woodhenge was built with wooden posts instead of stone slabs D where the bluestones used at Stonehenge actually came from	**8.9(A)**

Practice Test 5 • Prometheus the Fire Giver • How Maui Brought Fire to the World

Question & Answer	Standard
1 In paragraph 4 of "Prometheus the Fire Giver," the word <u>deliberation</u> means – A anxiety B disagreement C motivation **D thought**	**8.2(B)**
2 In "Prometheus the Fire Giver," paragraph 4 contributes to the rising action of the story by – F revealing the reasons for Kronos's exile **G presenting the problem Prometheus tries to solve** H introducing the conflict between Prometheus and Zeus J explaining why humans did not live up to Kronos's expectations	**8.6(A)**
3 Based on Prometheus's reaction to Zeus in paragraph 7 of "Prometheus the Fire Giver," what can be inferred about the gods? **A They were often in conflict with each other.** B They often abused their power. C They were not used to interacting with humans. D They caused most of the problems in the world.	**8.6(A)**
4 In "Prometheus the Fire Giver," paragraphs 8 and 9 contribute to the falling action of the story by showing that Zeus is – F worried that humans have become too powerful G eager to punish other gods **H angry that Prometheus has disobeyed him** J unwilling to compromise	**8.3(C)**

Question & Answer	Standard
5 In paragraph 9 of "How Maui Brought Fire to the World," the word *complied* means — A tried to assist **B met the demand** C made a sacrifice D wondered aloud	**8.2(B)**
6 In "How Maui Brought Fire to the World," what is the main problem? **F The villagers have no fire.** G No one will visit Mahuika. H Maui enrages Mahuika. J Maui loses the fire to the trees.	**8.6 Fig. 19(D)**
7 In "How Maui Brought Fire to the World," how does Maui's behavior influence the problem? A Maui's curiosity enables him to discover a solution to the villagers' problem. B Maui's lack of consideration prevents him from helping the villagers. **C Maui's childish behavior is the cause of the villagers' problem.** D Maui's close relationship with his grandmother allows him to solve the problem.	**8.6(B)**
8 In "How Maui Brought Fire to the World," how does the rising action help resolve the problem? F Maui's long journey reveals the difficulty of the task before him. **G Taranga's advice helps Maui discover the source of fire and escape with it.** H The villagers' fear of Mahuika foreshadows the outcome of the story. J Taranga makes sure Maui knows that his first obligation is to help the villagers.	**8.6(A)**

Question & Answer	Standard
9 Which sentence from "How Maui Brought Fire to the World" supports the warning Taranga gives Maui? A "Greetings, Grandson," said a deep and frightening voice from the darkness. "Why do you disturb me in my home?" B Mahuika liked her grandson and wanted to help the people, so she gave up another fingernail and sent him on his way. C Each time, he made up a new excuse and asked for another flame, and each time Mahuika complied by giving him another fingernail, and then a toenail, until finally she had only one left. **D That's when she realized that Maui had tricked her, and she became enraged.**	**8.6 Fig. 19(D)**
10 The trees in "How Maui Brought Fire to the World" are significant because they — F show Maui how fire first originated **G enable Maui to make his own fire** H save Maui from Mahuika's rage J provide shelter for the villagers	**8.3(C)**
11 The purpose in both of these selections is to — A explore the relationships among the deities **B explain where fire originally came from** C describe the hardships of life in ancient times **D** explain where humans originally came from	**8.3(B)**
12 Which is an accurate comparison of Maui and Prometheus in these two selections? F Both characters are sent on quests, but Prometheus's quest is unreasonable and Maui's is attainable. G Both characters disobey the advice they get, but Prometheus feels regretful and Maui does not. H Prometheus is embraced by humankind, but Maui is shunned by the villagers. **J Prometheus feels morally obligated to help humans, but Maui acts only for his personal satisfaction.**	**8.3(A)**

Question & Answer	Standard
13 Which of these elements is found in both myths? A The deities overstep their authority. **B The main character responds to a challenge.** C Nature causes a problem for humans. D Relationships among family members are tested.	**8.6 Fig. 19(F)**
14 In these two selections, both Zeus and Mahuika are – F helpful G unreasonable **H vengeful** J sympathetic	**8.3(B)**
15 Which thematic element is apparent in both myths? **A the importance of fire** B the existence of an afterlife C the value of listening to elders D the cruelty of nature	**8.3(A)**

Name____ Date____________

1 Ⓐ Ⓑ Ⓒ Ⓓ

2 Ⓕ Ⓖ Ⓗ Ⓙ

3 Ⓐ Ⓑ Ⓒ Ⓓ

4 Ⓕ Ⓖ Ⓗ Ⓙ

5 Ⓐ Ⓑ Ⓒ Ⓓ

6 Ⓕ Ⓖ Ⓗ Ⓙ

7 Ⓐ Ⓑ Ⓒ Ⓓ

8 Ⓕ Ⓖ Ⓗ Ⓙ

9 Ⓐ Ⓑ Ⓒ Ⓓ

10 Ⓕ Ⓖ Ⓗ Ⓙ

Name____ Date___________

1 Ⓐ Ⓑ Ⓒ Ⓓ

2 Ⓕ Ⓖ Ⓗ Ⓙ

3 Ⓐ Ⓑ Ⓒ Ⓓ

4 Ⓕ Ⓖ Ⓗ Ⓙ

5 Ⓐ Ⓑ Ⓒ Ⓓ

6 Ⓕ Ⓖ Ⓗ Ⓙ

7 Ⓐ Ⓑ Ⓒ Ⓓ

8 Ⓕ Ⓖ Ⓗ Ⓙ

9 Ⓐ Ⓑ Ⓒ Ⓓ

10 Ⓕ Ⓖ Ⓗ Ⓙ

Name____ Date____________

1 Ⓐ Ⓑ Ⓒ Ⓓ   11 Ⓐ Ⓑ Ⓒ Ⓓ

2 Ⓕ Ⓖ Ⓗ Ⓙ   12 Ⓕ Ⓖ Ⓗ Ⓙ

3 Ⓐ Ⓑ Ⓒ Ⓓ   13 Ⓐ Ⓑ Ⓒ Ⓓ

4 Ⓕ Ⓖ Ⓗ Ⓙ   14 Ⓕ Ⓖ Ⓗ Ⓙ

5 Ⓐ Ⓑ Ⓒ Ⓓ   15 Ⓐ Ⓑ Ⓒ Ⓓ

6 Ⓕ Ⓖ Ⓗ Ⓙ

7 Ⓐ Ⓑ Ⓒ Ⓓ

8 Ⓕ Ⓖ Ⓗ Ⓙ

9 Ⓐ Ⓑ Ⓒ Ⓓ

10 Ⓕ Ⓖ Ⓗ Ⓙ

Name____ Date___________

1 Ⓐ Ⓑ Ⓒ Ⓓ   11 Ⓐ Ⓑ Ⓒ Ⓓ

2 Ⓕ Ⓖ Ⓗ Ⓙ   12 Ⓕ Ⓖ Ⓗ Ⓙ

3 Ⓐ Ⓑ Ⓒ Ⓓ   13 Ⓐ Ⓑ Ⓒ Ⓓ

4 Ⓕ Ⓖ Ⓗ Ⓙ   14 Ⓕ Ⓖ Ⓗ Ⓙ

5 Ⓐ Ⓑ Ⓒ Ⓓ   15 Ⓐ Ⓑ Ⓒ Ⓓ

6 Ⓕ Ⓖ Ⓗ Ⓙ

7 Ⓐ Ⓑ Ⓒ Ⓓ

8 Ⓕ Ⓖ Ⓗ Ⓙ

9 Ⓐ Ⓑ Ⓒ Ⓓ

10 Ⓕ Ⓖ Ⓗ Ⓙ

Name____ Date____________

1 Ⓐ Ⓑ Ⓒ Ⓓ   11 Ⓐ Ⓑ Ⓒ Ⓓ

2 Ⓕ Ⓖ Ⓗ Ⓙ   12 Ⓕ Ⓖ Ⓗ Ⓙ

3 Ⓐ Ⓑ Ⓒ Ⓓ   13 Ⓐ Ⓑ Ⓒ Ⓓ

4 Ⓕ Ⓖ Ⓗ Ⓙ   14 Ⓕ Ⓖ Ⓗ Ⓙ

5 Ⓐ Ⓑ Ⓒ Ⓓ   15 Ⓐ Ⓑ Ⓒ Ⓓ

6 Ⓕ Ⓖ Ⓗ Ⓙ

7 Ⓐ Ⓑ Ⓒ Ⓓ

8 Ⓕ Ⓖ Ⓗ Ⓙ

9 Ⓐ Ⓑ Ⓒ Ⓓ

10 Ⓕ Ⓖ Ⓗ Ⓙ

Practice Test Form

Name____ Date__________

1 (A) (B) (C) (D)	1 (A) (B) (C) (D)	1 (A) (B) (C) (D)
2 (F) (G) (H) (J)	2 (F) (G) (H) (J)	2 (F) (G) (H) (J)
3 (A) (B) (C) (D)	3 (A) (B) (C) (D)	3 (A) (B) (C) (D)
4 (F) (G) (H) (J)	4 (F) (G) (H) (J)	4 (F) (G) (H) (J)
5 (A) (B) (C) (D)	5 (A) (B) (C) (D)	5 (A) (B) (C) (D)
6 (F) (G) (H) (J)	6 (F) (G) (H) (J)	6 (F) (G) (H) (J)
7 (A) (B) (C) (D)	7 (A) (B) (C) (D)	7 (A) (B) (C) (D)
8 (F) (G) (H) (J)	8 (F) (G) (H) (J)	8 (F) (G) (H) (J)
9 (A) (B) (C) (D)	9 (A) (B) (C) (D)	9 (A) (B) (C) (D)
10 (F) (G) (H) (J)	10 (F) (G) (H) (J)	10 (F) (G) (H) (J)
	11 (A) (B) (C) (D)	11 (A) (B) (C) (D)
	12 (F) (G) (H) (J)	12 (F) (G) (H) (J)
	13 (A) (B) (C) (D)	13 (A) (B) (C) (D)
	14 (F) (G) (H) (J)	14 (F) (G) (H) (J)
	15 (A) (B) (C) (D)	15 (A) (B) (C) (D)

Notes